Children at

Also available from Marshall Pickering by Rachel Stowe:

Women at Prayer

Forthcoming:

A Little Book of Women's Prayer

The Revd Canon Rachel Stowe is an Honorary Canon of St Albans Cathedral, and was recently elected a member of the Worldwide Council of the Mothers' Union, having spent five years as its Central Prayer Correspondent.

Rachel Stowe's ministry includes work with children in church groups, a women's refuge, Pram services, youth services and camps, and as a speaker at school assemblies and playgroups, and she still finds time to enjoy her three children and three grandchildren.

Rachel Stowe is the compiler of the enormously successful *Women at Prayer*, an anthology contributed to by members of the Mothers' Union throughout the world.

Children at Prayer

Compiled by Rachel Stowe

Marshall Pickering
An Imprint of HarperCollins*Publishers*

Marshall Pickering is an Imprint of
HarperCollins*Religious*
Part of HarperCollins*Publishers*
77–85 Fulham Palace Road, London W6 8JB

First published in Great Britain
in 1996 by Marshall Pickering

1   3   5   7   9   10   8   6   4   2

Copyright © 1996 in this compilation, Rachel Stowe

Rachel Stowe asserts the moral right to be
identified as the compiler of this work

A catalogue record for this book is
available from the British Library

0 551 03016X

Printed and bound in Great Britain by
Caledonian International Book Manufacturing Ltd, Glasgow, G64

CONDITIONS OF SALE
This book is sold subject to the condition that it
shall not, by way of trade or otherwise, be lent, re-sold,
hired out or otherwise circulated without the publisher's
prior consent in any form of binding or cover other
than that in which it is published and without a
similar condition including this condition being
imposed on the subsequent purchaser.

All rights reserved. No part of this publication may be
reproduced, stored in a retrieval system, or transmitted,
in any form or by any means, electronic, mechanical,
photocopying, recording or otherwise, without the prior
permission of the publishers.

Contents

How to Use This Book	vi
Introduction	vii
The Months – Sara Coleridge	ix
January	1
February	15
March	27
April	41
May	53
June	67
July	79
August	93
September	105
October	119
November	131
December	143
Index	159
Acknowledgements	166

How to Use This Book

All these prayers have been written by children between the ages of three and nine, but they can be used by people of any age.

There is an index at the back of *Children at Prayer*, so if you want to find a prayer about school look under 'S' or if you want one for your family look under 'F' and so on. Or why not start using this book by looking up the prayer for the day of your birthday and use that? Or if that isn't what you want look at the day before, or the day after, until you find the right one for you. Or start with the prayer written for the actual day you are looking at the book. Some of you might want to use every prayer, but don't feel you have to. Use the ones that say what you want to say and if you want to change some of the words please do.

You can use these prayers at home, at school, at church, with your group; on your own or with others. They are there to help you talk to God, at any time and in any place.

Introduction

Jesus clearly thought that children matter. He said to his disciples, 'Let the children come to me and don't send them away, because the Kingdom of God belongs to such as these. I tell you that anyone who does not come to God like a little child will never enter his Kingdom.'

What a marvellous collection of prayers you sent in! Thank you all, and I wish I could have included every single one for they all had something special to say to God. Over 3800 prayers came in from all over England, Scotland, Ireland and Wales (and one from Belgium). Amongst them was an entry from seven-year-old Jessica Penther of Sywell C of E School in Northamptonshire. She calls it 'Talking to God' and I thought her words were so good I would use them in this introduction. 'When we talk to God it is called a prayer. There is no particular time to talk to God. If you think that you can only talk to God in church and assemblies you are wrong, because you can talk to God at any time you want. You are often saying thank you to God, but that is not the only thing you can say to God. You can say how happy you are or how sad you are or even how thankful you are, for God listens to everything we say.'

When we pray we are simply telling God about all

the things that are important to us and he will always answer us. He may not always say 'yes' because he may think it right to say 'no' or 'not yet'. We have to listen carefully and perhaps wait for a while before he does answer, but God is always there for us. Although sometimes he might be disappointed about some of the wrong things we do he always loves us and wants us to do the best we can. So we can praise him, ask him for help, ask him to care for those we love. We can say sorry for the things we are ashamed of and promise to do better in future and he will forgive us. As Jessica says, we can talk to God at any time we want.

The verses I have used from the Bible have been put into everyday language, but if you want to read more about God and Jesus you can look them up yourself. I'm sure your vicar or minister or teacher or group leader or member of your family will always help you.

When a member of Hensingham Explorers Group in Cumbria was asked why she liked books of prayer she replied, 'It makes me think of other things in my life I want to talk to Jesus and God about.' I hope that *Children at Prayer* will help you do the same.

The Months

JANUARY brings the snow,
Makes our feet and fingers glow.

FEBRUARY brings the rain,
Thaws the frozen lake again.

MARCH brings breezes loud and shrill,
Stirs the dancing daffodil.

APRIL brings the primrose sweet,
Scatters daisies at our feet.

MAY brings flocks of pretty lambs,
Skipping by their fleecy dams.

JUNE brings tulips, lilies, roses,
Fills the children's hands with posies.

Hot JULY brings cooling showers,
Apricots and gillyflowers.

AUGUST brings the sheaves of corn,
Then the harvest home is borne.

Warm SEPTEMBER brings the fruit,
Sportsmen then begin to shoot.

Fresh OCTOBER brings the pheasant,
Then to gather nuts is pleasant.

Dull NOVEMBER brings the blast,
Then the leaves are whirling fast.

Chill DECEMBER brings the sleet,
Blazing fire, and Christmas treat.

Sara Coleridge (1802–52)

January brings the snow,
Makes our feet and fingers glow

The best way to start a new year is by praising God.
'Praise him from sunrise to sunset' *Psalm 113:3*

January 1st

Thank you God for happy sunny days,
And helping us in all different ways.
Thank you God for gloomy rainy days,
And being there for me, always.

Jennifer Hobbs (8) All Hallows' Church Explorers, Allerton, Liverpool.

and then we ask Him to look after us:

January 2nd – a 'pyramid' prayer

Lord
Keep me safe
Through all the long years
Jesus, love me for ever.
Jesus, our Lord, for ever. Amen.

Kirsty Smith (8) St Thomas' Mustard Seeds Junior Church, Thurstonland, West Yorkshire.

The New Year is a time when we can decide to make a fresh start, knowing that God is always there to help us if we ask him to.

January 3rd

Dear Father, please help us not to do wrong things. Help us learn from all our mistakes. Then, help us to forget about the wrong things we do one day so the next day can have a fresh start. Thank you God for all the beautiful surroundings of the world. Help us not to take it for granted, but instead help us to look after it.

Jonathan Prescott (8) St David's Church, Haigh, Lancashire.

January 4th

Dear Father God, please help us to care for other people, to be kind and helpful and do what we are told. Please help us to look after things and help us to be careful with our pets.

Megan Woodrow (5) Ringwood C of E Infant School, Hampshire.

January 5th

Hi God, please will you help me to be brave and try new things, like going on a roller coaster? Thank you God for helping me. I love you.

Philip Anderson (8) Billinge St Aidan's C of E Primary School, Merseyside.

January 6th

EPIPHANY is when we think about the Wise Men coming to visit Jesus and to worship him. This made King Herod very angry and Mary, Joseph and Jesus had to leave their home and go to Egypt. (You can read all about this in the Bible in Matthew chapter 2.)

Dear Lord, thank you for loving us and giving us the power to love each other as well as loving you. Your love is like a never ending doorway to freedom, so please help our love to grow as strong as yours and as never ending as yours. I'm sorry if I hurt your feelings sometimes, and help me to love you more than I do now. Help everyone to become a Christian and let love be a thing that will last over time and never end.

Craig Wood (8) Riseley C of E Lower School, Bedfordshire.

January 7th

Please God, will you keep my family safe always? I thank you Lord.

Stephen Edghill (6) Monasterevan, Co. Kildare.

January 8th
Dear God, please let the world find peace very soon. Please help the richer people give more generously to the poorer people, here and in other countries. Help people to live beside one another even when they have a different religion, and be happy and peaceful always.

Anna McLean (8) Bearsden Primary School, Glasgow.

January 9th
Thank you God for our new baby. Thank you God for making us.

Daisy Pogson-Browne (5) St Mary's Infant School, Hornsey, London.

> At the start of a new school term, we ask God to help us.
>> 'Listen carefully to what you are taught and you will do well' Proverbs 16:20

January 10th
Dear God, help us to do better work and to be good and kind, and to tidy up the messes we make.

Jennifer Padgett (5) St Thomas the Martyr School, Upholland, Lancashire.

January 11th
Father God, thank you for the churches and all the teachers. Thank you that they help us to learn about you. Please help us to remember what we are taught and help us to put it into practice.
Samantha Sharp (8) St Peter & St Paul Sunday School, Caistor, Lincolnshire.

January 12th
Dear God, Sunday is your special day. We go to church and we sing songs and we learn about Jesus. I like Sundays. Thank you God.
Daniel Martin Ward (4) All Saints' Church, Hindley, Lancashire.

January 13th
Dear Jesus, I thank you for my eyes. My eyes are for looking at the Bible and teaching me all about you. Thank you.
Sarah McCelland (8) Annaghmore Parish Sunday School, Co. Armagh.

and there are lots of things we can thank God for:

January 14th
Thank you God for a
- F　amily that loves me
- A　ll things they give me
- M　any times they help me
- I　mportant days they never forget.
- L　ove and care they show me
- Y　esterday, today and tomorrow.

Wendy Honner (8) Mountrath, Co. Laoise.

January 15th
Thank you God for a lovely day today.

Jonathan Clatworthy (5) Witney Parish Church Sunday Schools, Oxfordshire.

January 16th
Dear God, thank you for the happy times at home, at school and at play. Giving thanks and sharing good things brings a happy face. Thank you for all happy children; sharing and caring makes people happy.

Emma Booth (9) St Mary's Church, Gomersal, West Yorkshire.

January 17th
Dear Lord, thank you for friends who walk home with me; thank you for friends who play with me; thank you for friends who live close to me. Please make me a good friend too.

Katrina Ellis (9) St John's Junior Church, High Wycombe, Buckinghamshire.

January 18th
Dear God, thank you for my home, and for looking after the world and everyone in the world, and looking after me.

Laura Carter (5) St Mary's Sunday School, Wigton, Cumbria.

January 19th
Dear God, thank you for all the Brownies, Guides, Scouts, Cubs, Rainbows and Beavers all over the world. Thank you for all who stand by me when I am sick or need help. Please care for them just as they do for me.

Claire Markey (9) 6th Huyton Parish Brownies, Huyton, Merseyside.

January 20th
Dear Lord, thank you for light and dark, for sleep and awake, but most of all for love.

Kelly Brentnall (7) St Peter's School, Pedmore, West Midlands.

> And now some prayers for other people, especially those who are ill.
>
> 'Pray for one another, so that you will be healed'
> James 5:16

January 21st
Dear Father God, today there are many children all over the world who cannot get up because they are sick. Some of them have been ill for a long time and have forgotten what it is like to run and play and enjoy games with their friends. Lord, help us to imagine what it is like to stay in bed all the time and how lonely it must feel. Help us to think what we can do for anyone we know who is ill. In Jesus' name.

Julia Sarah Hynes (7) St Thomas the Martyr, Upholland, Lancashire.

January 22nd
Dear Lord Jesus, please will you make my friend better. He is very ill in hospital and hardly ever comes out.

Kathryn Almond (4) St Francis' Church, Orrell, Wigan, Lancashire.

or handicapped in some way

January 23rd
Dear Jesus, please help my friend to hear properly
and not talk baby noises.
*Charlotte Rebecca Topham (5) St James the Less Sunday
School, Penicuik, Edinburgh.*

or dying:

January 24th
Dear Lord, please help people who are
dying from sickness and sorrow. Dear Lord,
help everybody around the world.
*Gareth Thomas (7) St John's Sunday School, Alltwen, Cilybebyll,
West Glamorgan.*

January 25th
This is the day when we think about St Paul
becoming a Christian.

'I am Jesus, whom you persecute,' the voice
said, 'but get up and go into the city, where you
will be told what you must do' Acts 9:5 and 6

Lord, you know what I am thinking. You know what is best for me. Whatever happens, I want to please you.
Debbie Tinker (8) St Peter & St Paul Sunday School, Caistor, Lincolnshire.

Some prayers about looking after God's world:

January 26th
Dear God, thank you for our animals. Help us to look after them properly by keeping our animals clean, feeding them and keeping them warm in winter.
Rebecca Roberts (6) Lightcliffe C of E School, Halifax, West Yorkshire.

January 27th
Dear God, help us to understand that we only have one world and if we destroy it there will be nothing left. Help us to learn to care for all living things so that everybody can enjoy the beauty of the world.
Katie Proctor (8) Harlaxton Sunday School, Lincolnshire.

January 28th

Dear God, please help us to clean up the country. People are terrible at dumping rubbish all over everywhere, and the traffic fumes are polluting our environment. And please help us to stop people killing animals for their skins or they will soon become extinct.

Hannah Wallace (8) St Saviour's Sunday School, Raynes Park, London.

January 29th

Dear God of us all, there are lots of people who need your help. There are people all over the world who need food and water. There are people all over the world who have no homes and have to live outside without shelter. There are children all over the world without a mummy or daddy or anyone to adopt them. Please God help all the people who need your help. Help me to be kind and helpful and keep the Brownie Guide law.

Katharine Hughes (8) 6th Huyton Brownies, Huyton, Merseyside.

January 30th
Thank you Lord for our good food. Help me not to waste anything and to think about people who are poorer than me. I promise to look after the world and all its wonderful gifts.

Stephen O'Shea (9) Selwood Anglican/Methodist Middle School, Frome, Somerset.

January 31st
Dear God, well done for making the world and all creatures. You are incredible, amazing and great. Thank you for helping us when we are ill and in trouble. Thank you for January, February, March, April, May, June, July, August, September, October, November and December.

Calvin Jenkins (9) St Brides Major Church in Wales Primary School, Mid Glamorgan.

February brings the rain,
Thaws the frozen lake again

The days are short and the nights are dark
but both light and dark are gifts of God.

February 1st

Dear Father in heaven, thank you for the life you have given us and the animals you have made. Thank you for light and dark. If there were no light we would not be able to see. And if there were no dark we would not be able to sleep. Thank you for everything you have given us.

Rachael Cordingley (8) St Gabriel's C of E Primary School, Huyton, Merseyside.

February 2nd

> Today we think about when Jesus was a baby and his parents took him to the Temple.
>> 'Jesus's parents took him up to Jerusalem to present him to the Lord' Luke 2:22

Dear God, thank you for church. It helps me to learn about you. It is a place where we come every Sunday to sing and pray to God.

Peter Smyth (9) Aghadowey Parish Sunday School, Coleraine.

February 3rd

Dear God, thank you for babies who are so wonderfully made, for their tiny hands and feet, their tiny nails, their soft skin and warm smell. Help us to be very gentle with them.

Eleanor Postlethwaite (9) St Paul's Explorers, Barrow-in-Furness, Cumbria.

Some people have no homes to live in and in winter it gets very cold and dark:

February 4th

Dear Jesus, we are sorry that people are lonely. Lots of people on the streets are lonely. They have no money, no food, no nice clothes, no warmth, no homes. We hope that they will find some friends. Please look after all the lonely people.

Emma Wilcox (7) St Mary's Church, Gomersal, West Yorkshire.

February 5th
Dear God, thank you for our friends and family, and I pray that you will bless them all. Thank you for food to eat, a bed to sleep in, clothes to wear, and best of all, your love. I pray that you will be with people who are less fortunate than us; people who are homeless, people who are living in a place where there is war or lots of fighting, and people who are ill.
Grace Farringdon (8) Childwall C of E School and Frontline Church, Liverpool.

so we give thanks for our families and friends:

February 6th
Dear Jesus, babies cry and mummies come. Toddlers crawl and learn to walk. Children play and run around. Teenagers grow up and turn into adults. Grown-ups get married and sometimes have babies. They become grannies and grandpas. And this is the family tree. Good Jesus, look after us.
Olivia Walmsley (7) Ryhall Church, Stamford, Lincolnshire.

February 7th
Dear God, families are fun sometimes, families are miserable sometimes, families laugh and play together, sometimes they argue. But families always care. Thank you God.
James Rodgers (8) St Mary's Church, Felpham, West Sussex.

February 8th
Dear God, thank you for my family. Where would I be without them? Thank you for my relations and help to keep them safe from harm. Help us to be kind and loving to each other. God bless everyone.
Greta Gormley (8) St Nicholas National School, Galway.

especially for our parents:

February 9th
Thank you God for my dad. He takes me to the park and he pushes me on the swings.
John Hicklin (6) St Thomas C of E Primary School, Lydiate, Merseyside.

February 10th
Dear God, thank you for my mam's kisses and cuddles.
John Jardine (5) Bishop Goodwin Infant School, Carlisle, Cumbria.

and grandparents:

February 11th
Thank you God for my grandad. He gives me lots of smiles.
Adam Gee (6) St Thomas C of E Primary School, Lydiate, Merseyside.

February 12th
Thank you God for my kind nan. She cooks nice cakes and food.
James Haslam (5) Longview Primary School, Huyton, Merseyside.

and great-grandparents:

February 13th
Thank you God for making my great-grandma be alive in both of the wars. Please God make me like my great-grandma.
Charlotte Henderson (5) Newburgh C of E School, Lancashire.

February 14th
Today is St Valentine's Day when we think about those we love most.

Dear God, thank you for St Valentine's Day
to appreciate other people and to send love, to
help other people to love and have fun. Please
help me to love. For Jesus' sake.
Michael James Ellis (8) Read C of E School, Burnley, Lancashire.

Sometimes we worry about our families:

February 15th
Dear Father God, please be with Mum and make her better.
Nicholas (6) and Matthew (5) Warmoth, St Peter & St Paul Sunday School, Caistor, Lincolnshire.

February 16th
Dear God, I am worried about my dad as he does a lot of driving each day. And my brother who is under a lot of medication and my sister who is finding some sport a bit hard. Please look after everything Lord.
Allan Treacy (8) Castlecomer, Co. Kilkenny.

February 17th
Dear God, please save my grandad because he is very very sick, and I do not know what I will do without my grandad.
James Byford (8) St Peter's School, Formby, Merseyside.

February 18th

Dear God, we know that you love us and we know that we love you. We pray for our mum and dad and especially for my brother because he is handicapped and he cannot pray for himself. As we pray I would like you to remember my grannies, grandpa, aunts, uncles and cousins. Help us all to live happily together.

Kim Dennison (6) Ballymore Parish, Armagh diocese.

> and sometimes we need help:
> 'God is our shelter and strength, always ready to help in times of trouble' Psalm 46:1

February 19th

Dear Lord, help us to do what is best. Help us to understand the ways of life. Help us to learn how to serve you and to overcome our problems. In the name of Jesus Christ our Lord.

Samuel Marrlew (7) St Thomas, Westfield Street, St Helens, Merseyside.

February 20th

Dear Father God, please help the people I love. Please help me when I am hurt.

Danny Goodridge (7) Matlock All Saints' Infants School, Derbyshire.

February 21st

Dear Lord, please help the people who are lonely or sad. Please comfort the families who have had their children die.

Zoe Jenkin (9) St Paul's Explorers, Barrow-in-Furness, Cumbria.

February 22nd

Dear God, please help me when I feel sad. Please make me happy when I am sad so I can cheer up my friends.

Catherine Mary-Ann Pash (8) The Seekers Group, St George's Church, Fovant, Wiltshire.

February 23rd

Thank you Jesus, you knew that I was a little bit nervous. You knew this and you made me feel a lot better.

Laura Mulholland (6) Roberttown C of E School, West Yorkshire.

at school:

February 24th

Dear Holy Father, this is a prayer for help. Dear God, help me at school when I work in class, and please help me at home too. Thank you for giving us life.

Leah Crockett (8) Longview Primary School, Huyton, Merseyside.

February 25th
Dear God, please help us to be brave, help us to be tidy, help us not to be selfish. Help us to share things, help us to like each other person.
Megan Woodrow (5) Ringwood C of E Infant School, Hampshire.

February 26th
Dear Lord, when my friends get on my nerves help me to keep calm. Help me to be friends with them and sort it out without getting upset.
Nicola Nevill (9) The Seekers Group, St George's Church, Fovant, Wiltshire.

February 27th
Dear Lord, help me to think before I do something. Help me to work better in lessons and to listen. Thank you for who I am and for my life.
Alison Earle (9) Selwood Anglican/Methodist Middle School, Frome, Somerset.

and at home:

February 28th

Dear God,   Keep us safe every day
Keep the bad things far away.
Look after my family and my friends,
Give them love that never ends.
Thank you for all we have to share,
God, spread your love everywhere!

Laura Gibbons (8) Parcroft County Junior School, Yeovil, Somerset.

February 29th

In the name of the Father and of the Son and of the Holy Spirit. Dear God, help me and my family and friends be happier people.

Gemma Copley (8) St Pius Brownies, Grimsby, Humberside.

March brings breezes loud and shrill, Stirs the dancing daffodil

'Stop and listen and consider the wonderful things God does' *Job 37:14*

March 1st

St David is the patron saint of Wales so today we have a prayer from Wales.

Thank you God for the world to stand on. Please help us look after it.
Fiona Winslade (5) St Andrews Major C in W Primary School, South Glamorgan.

Spring is coming so we thank God for his beautiful world.
'O Lord, our Lord, your greatness is seen in all the world!' Psalm 8:1

March 2nd

Thank you Lord for the warm spring. Thank you Lord for the summer sunshine and for the rich autumn and the snow to play in in winter. Thank you Lord for giving us all this playful weather.
Helen Robinson (8) Morpeth Parish Church, Northumberland.

March 3rd

Dear God, thank you for the moon, the stars and the earth you have lent us. Please help us to make the world a better place than it is at the moment, and please let there be peace in the world.
St Mary's Explorers (ages 7–10) Horsham, West Sussex.

March 4th

Dear Lord, thank you for our lovely world, as beautiful as can be. I go for a walk, see lovely plants and birds that sing, and the sea that twinkles in the sunshine and the mountains that look like they touch the sky. Thank you for making all of these things.

Hannah Mainey (7) St John's Explorers, Hensingham, Whitehaven, Cumbria.

March 5th

Dear God, thank you for all the different weather — sun, rain, wind and snow.

Kayleigh Walton (7) Wantage C of E Infants School, Oxfordshire.

March 6th

Dear God, thank you for the colours of the rainbow, yellow and red and orange and blue and the other colours. They make our world a nicer place.

Gary Schofield (7) Read C of E School, Burnley, Lancashire.

But sometimes we don't look after God's world very well:

March 7th
Dear God, bless all the teachers who help us learn about caring for our world. It is not very nice to see pollution. Help us to recycle our rubbish in the recycling bins for we know it won't get recycled left on the ground; instead it will look untidy and may cause an accident. Help people to stop using cars and other vehicles too much because of the fumes that can cause very bad illnesses.

Louise Harris (8) The Beacon Primary School, Exmouth, Devon.

March 8th
Dear God, please help us to stop people dropping litter on the beach for the birds are catching their feet on the cans. Please help us to stop cutting down the trees so that we can all breathe better and see the animals who live in them.

Tom Scobie (7) St Mary's C of E Infant School, Prestbury, Gloucestershire.

March 9th
Dear God, please help the environment and stop people from wasting electricity and from dumping rubbish.

Josephine Emma Hannan (8) St Saviour's Sunday School, Raynes Park, London.

March 10th

Dear God, thank you for water but please stop people from using too much. We need to share water instead of being greedy. Please help us to remember those who do not have enough clean water. Help the workers who are bringing clean water to villages in Africa and help us not to take clean water for granted.

Gary Brooke (8) St Mary's Church, Gomersal, West Yorkshire.

> LENT is a time when we say sorry for the wrong things we have done and promise to try and be more like Jesus.
>
> 'You are to be perfect, just as your Father in heaven is perfect' Matthew 5:48

March 11th

Dear Father, forgive me for all the bad things I have done, and help me forgive those who have done bad things to me. Help me to get over it. Help me to tell people all about you.

Adam Oakley (9) St Paul's Church, Skelmersdale, Lancashire.

March 12th
Dear Lord, help us to say sorry when we have done something wrong, been nasty or hurt someone or done something that we know is wrong. Sorry means that we really are very sorry for doing something wrong, and that we will try never to do it again.

Gregory Simkin (7) St Nicholas Sunday School, Codsall, Staffordshire.

March 13th
Sorry, God, I have made a mistake.

Richard Booth (6) Roberttown C of E School, Liversedge, West Yorkshire.

March 14th
Dear God, help us to be kind and loving to our mums, dads, friends and teachers. We are sorry because sometimes we don't have time for them.

Sarah Hall (7) 10th Wigan West (St Francis) Brownies, Wigan, Lancashire.

March 15th

Sorry God that sometimes I'm not helpful when I could be helpful. Sorry God that sometimes I am careless. Help me to do better next time. Sorry God when I do not share. Help me to do better.

Katherine Michie (8) St James' Junior Church, Morpeth, Northumberland.

March 16th

Dear Lord, teach us to be quick to hear the voice inside that warns us when we are doing wrong. May we always be ready to obey it. For Jesus' sake.

Joanna Hobbs (8) Eythorne Benefice Junior Quest, Shepherdswell, Dover, Kent.

March 17th

ST PATRICK is the patron saint of Ireland, so today we have a prayer from Ireland.

Father we thank you for the night,
And for the pleasant morning light,
For rest and food and loving care,
And all that makes the day so fair.

Helen Lyttle (9) Annaghmore Parish Sunday School, Co. Armagh.

We thank God for all those who teach us about Jesus.
  'Jesus travelled around the towns and villages, teaching and preaching' Matthew 9:35

March 18th
Dear God, thank you for our homes and families, and thank you for our teachers and Vicars and Sunday School teachers. We pray that you will keep them in your love and your care and we hope that you will help the people who haven't even got one of them.
Rebecca Broughton (7) St David's Church, Carr Mill, St Helens, Merseyside.

March 19th
Heavenly Father, teach everyone to listen, understand and remember the things we are told in church. When we pray let it be just like talking to you. Help us to remember what is said, so that we can go out and tell other people what we have learned in your house.
13th St Mary's Beaver Colony (6–8 years) Far Cotton, Northampton.

March 20th
Dear God, thank you for all the churches and choirs, and for all the songs people have written.
Nadine Gallimore (8) St Mary's Parish Church, Prescot, Merseyside.

March 21st
Dear Lord Jesus, we pray for priests and missionaries and for the way they use their time. They don't get much money for doing their job, but they do it for you, Lord Jesus, because they love you like you love us.
Laura Smith (9) Riseley C of E Lower School, Bedfordshire.

and for our church buildings:
> 'The believers met together regularly' Acts 2:44

March 22nd
We thank you Lord for our church, for this beautiful building, for worship and prayer, praising and thanksgiving, for our coffee and biscuits after the service, for fellowship and friendship.
Emily Stelfox (7) St Anne's Church, Ings, Cumbria.

March 23rd
Dear God, thank you for our friends and family, and our world and our church.
Jonathan Board (5) St Paul's Sunday School, Honiton, Devon.

And most of all, we thank God for Jesus:

March 24th
Dear God, thank you for your son Jesus, who taught us a lot about you.
Kay Hoyle (8) Holy Trinity Church, South Crosland, West Yorkshire.

March 25th
Today is Lady Day, when we think about the Angel Gabriel telling Mary she was going to have a very special baby called Jesus.

'The angel said to her "Don't be afraid, Mary; God has been gracious to you. You will become pregnant and give birth to a son, and you will name him Jesus. He will be great and will be called the Son of the Most High God".' Luke 1:30, 31 and 32

Mothering Sunday is often about this time, when we thank God for our own mothers:

Dear Father in heaven, we thank you for all the mothers in the world, for all their love and care each day and for all the work they do for us. We pray for mothers who are sick on this special day.
Lynsay Bruffell (7) St Anne's Church, Aigburth, Liverpool.

We give thanks for all families:

March 26th
Dear God, thank you for minding me in the adoption centre and for giving me loving parents. Thank you for giving me such a nice family.
Jill Wright (9) Clane, Co. Kildare.

and pray for them:

March 27th
Dear God, help my dad to be safe in Bosnia. Help him to come to me. When he comes keep him safe and help him to get a job. Please God, help me, my mum and my sister to learn the language better and keep us safe in England and stop war in Bosnia.
Miran Serdarevic (8) Rainhill St Ann's Primary School, Liverpool.

March 28th
Thank you for my mum, and bless all the children with only one parent. Love them and help them in any way you can, for we know your love never ends.
Janet Louise Allen (8) Tubbercurry, Co. Sligo.

March 29th
Dear Lord, thank you for my friends and my family. Please help those who have no mummy and daddy and stop them from being sad.
Scott Latta (6) St Gabriel's C of E School, Huyton, Merseyside.

March 30th
Thank you, God our Father, for mums, dads, grannies and grandads, for brothers and sisters. Thank you for all the fun we enjoy. Helps us not to squabble and fight too much; we really need to help each other. Please help us to be kind and share our love with little boys and girls who do not know what family life is. Please help me when I sometimes find it hard to share my toys with little foster children who come to stay in my home. Help me to teach them how to pray and put their trust in you. For Jesus' sake.
Benjamin Sinnamon (8) Altedesert Parish, Armagh diocese.

March 31st

Lord Jesus, our homes are very special to us. They are places where our families live and where we feel loved and safe. Thank you for our mums and dads who work hard to give us a happy home. Sometimes we are so busy playing we forget to say thank you to them; please help us to try and remember. Home is where our brothers and sisters are, and where we can bring our friends to play. Home is where we have our toys and games. Home is where we can talk about things that go right and things that go wrong. Home is where we feel happy. Thank you for our homes.

Children from Witney Parish Sunday Schools, Oxfordshire.

April brings the primrose sweet, Scatters daisies at our feet

The days are getting longer, the flowers and trees
and plants are growing so we praise God for his creation.
'Let everything alive praise the Lord' *Psalm 150*

April 1st
Thank you God for day and night
Thank you God for dark and light
Thank you God for food and drink
Thank you God for everything.

Thank you God for all the flowers
I could say thank you for hours and hours.
Thank you for the birds that sing
Thank you God for everything.
Laura Woodcock (8) 5th Roby (Court Hey Methodist) Brownies, Liverpool.

April 2nd
Dear Jesus, thank you for making the world for us, and thank you for making all the things in the world.
Klara Wertheim (6) St Andrew's Sunday School, Shrivenham, Wiltshire.

April 3rd
Dear Lord, thank you for the seeds so we can have beautiful flowers.
Debbie Costain (6) St Michael in the Hamlet with St Andrew Girls Friendly Society, Liverpool.

April 4th
Dear God, thank you for all the flowers and trees. Thank you for water to make them grow, and for the farmers for giving us food.
Ruairi Campbell (7) Church of the Good Shepherd, Hillington, Glasgow.

April 5th
Dear Lord, thank you for all the animals in the world that walk, run, hop, swim, crawl, fly and slither.
April Dunham (8) St Mary's C of E School, Hornsey, London.

April 6th
Dear Lord, please look after the ladybirds and butterflies. They make us feel nice because they tell us when it is Spring.
Carolyn Forrester (7) Bishop Goodwin Infant School, Carlisle, Cumbria.

April 7th
Dear Lord, for all the birds that sing and fly and soar across the great blue sky, from giant eagle to tiny wren, we thank you very much.
Rachel McGowan (7) St Lawrence's Church, Kirkdale, Liverpool.

April 8th
Dear God, look after the sea and the fishes. Don't let anybody throw rubbish in the sea.
David Mawdsley (4) Ringwood C of E Infant School, Hampshire.

> This is usually the time of year when we think about Jesus, especially on Good Friday, when he died upon the cross, and Easter Day, when he rose from the dead. (You can read about it in the Bible in Mark chapters 14, 15 and 16.)

April 9th
Dear Jesus, when you lived on earth you had friends. Twelve of them loved you so much that they left everything and followed you. One of them betrayed you; his name was Judas. You know how to love those who hurt you and you know they are special. Thank you for friends. Let us never quarrel. If it is my fault let me say sorry and be forgiven by you.
Charlotte Masefield (9) Holy Trinity Church Club, Wednesfield Heath, West Midlands.

April 10th

Dear God, thank you for Jesus Christ, your son, who let himself be killed to save our lives. May we be as loving and as kind as he. I ask this in Jesus' name.

Felicity Evans (8) St John's Junior Church, High Wycombe, Buckinghamshire.

April 11th

Loving healing hands of Jesus, cruelly pierced for us on the cross. Thank you for the helping hands of Simon, taking the weight, and for Joseph's caring hands. Forgive those who nailed you to the cross. May our hands be lovely and caring like yours.

Children from St Oswald's Church, Sheffield, South Yorkshire.

April 12th

Dear Lord Jesus, I love you and praise you for dying on the cross. You were whipped and nails were put through your hands and feet. You did this for me. Thank you.

Owen Rhys Jones (7) St Mary's Sunday School, Grassendale, Liverpool.

April 13th
Dear Lord God, thank you for sending your son Jesus Christ to help and lead us, to forgive our sins and give us a new life. Thank you for being so brave.

Chloe Naylor (9) Crosby Ravensworth School, Penrith, Cumbria.

April 14th
Dear Lord, thank you for sending your son down to tell people about you, and thank you Jesus for dying for us. All the Christians in the world are very grateful. Lord, we thank you. Help us to tell other people about you and to spread the good news about you and how you died for us.

Zoe Bloodworth (9) Riseley C of E Lower School, Bedfordshire.

April 15th
Dear God, thank you for Easter time and all the churches around the world. Thank you for Easter eggs, and families and friends, and most important thank you for the world.

Mark James Wilson (7) Ormskirk C of E Primary School, Lancashire.

April 16th

Dear God, thank you for Easter and for Jesus who died for me. Thank you for all your wonderful creatures, newborn lambs and calves and ducklings; for pretty plants, yellow daffodils; for the warmth, light and water to make plants grow. But most of all thank you for your world and all the love in the world.

Hannah Mottershead (7) St Saviour's Church, Hagley, West Midlands.

> Sadly there are many places in the world where there is war:

April 17th

Dear Lord Jesus, we thank you for food, families, friends, animals and plants. Without all these things we could not live. We ask you Lord to heal the world now of war and famine.

Victoria Lewis (7) St Paul's Explorers, Barrow-in-Furness, Cumbria.

April 18th

Dear Lord, I hope we don't have any more wars or people setting bombs off.

Thomas Wardle (7) 10th Warrington St Mary's Beavers, Cheshire.

April 19th
Dear God, please help us to stop the fighting all over the world. Help us to remember what war is, and do something about it. All of us argue, but this world would be much nicer with harmony. In Jesus' name.
Rachael Elizabeth Atkinson (9) St Mark's C of E Primary School, Wigan, Lancashire.

April 20th
Dear Father, please will you be with the people in the wars. Please be with the families that are hurt, poor, lonely and ill. Help the people find homes, food and water. Please make the fighting stop and please be with the relatives whose families have been killed or died.
Hannah Walker (9) Latham St James C of E School, Ormskirk, Lancashire.

April 21st
Dear God, please let the world carry on as it is, but in a more peaceful way. Let everybody learn to love one another and stop arguing and fighting. It is important to have friends, because if you didn't the world would be a dark and lonely planet. Thank you Lord.
Leah Gasson (8) The Beacon Primary School, Exmouth, Devon.

April 22nd
Dear God, please help those people in other countries who have nothing to eat and nothing to drink. Please deliver some food and fresh water and help people who are ill. Please stop the fighting, and bless all the good people and forgive the bad people.

Michael Lee (7) St Thomas the Martyr Church, Upholland, Lancashire.

April 23rd
ST GEORGE is the patron saint of England, so today we have a prayer from England.

Dear Father, although I am only small I understand about the problems in the third world countries. Help me to help others to understand also. Thank you for keeping us safe in our country and keep the Queen safe so that she can look after us too.

Victoria Sweeney (7) St Mark's Church, Oldham, Lancashire.

April 24th
Dear Lord, I pray to you this very moment for what you have done for us today. Everybody in the world should pray to you and perhaps they will one day.

Amy Bugler (9) Christ Church, Redhill, Wrington, Bristol, Avon.

We ask God to help us care for each other:

April 25th
Dear God, help us to be helpful and good and to be nice to people, and to serve you and everyone else, and to help people if they are in pain.
Stephen Nightingale (7) Matlock All Saints' Infants School, Matlock, Derbyshire.

April 26th
Dear God, please help us to be polite to people, and help us to be kind and helpful to other people too.
Natalie Wilkinson (8) 1st Prescot Brownies, Prescot, Merseyside.

You can use the letters of your name to write a prayer – why not try it with your name?

April 27th
- J esus please help me to be good
- O n Sunday please help me not to work too hard
- N ot to be silly or stupid
- A nd to help my friends
- T hat I play with
- H elp me to be helpful
- A nd pray every day and
- N ever be horrid to animals

Jonathan Russell (9) Stoke Gabriel Sunday Club, Totnes, Devon.

April 28th

Dear Lord, I thank you for my heart and my feelings. Help us not to be cruel to one another and not to hurt other people's feelings. Help us not to be hurtful to nature and the creatures you, God, have made.

Matthew Siggsworth (8) Saleshurst Sunday Club, East Sussex.

April 29th

Dear Jesus, you loved everyone, even those who were unkind to you. Help us to try very hard to be the same. Thank you for all the good things you give to us, especially our family and our friends.

Carina Hartshorne (6) St James' Sunday School, Chapelthorpe, West Yorkshire.

April 30th

Dear Lord, thank you for the food we eat and for the clothes on our back. We are sorry when we grumble. Please let us understand how fortunate we are, and help us to think about the less fortunate. Help us to understand all about you and believe in you. Please help there to be peace in the world, and help us to understand each other, to love each other and to care about others.

Desreen Burrell (9) St Stephen's Sunday School, Norbury, London.

May brings flocks of pretty lambs,
Skipping by their fleecy dams

We give thanks for the whole universe.
'God looked at everything he had made,
and he was very pleased' *Genesis 1:31*

May 1st

Hear all the birds singing
And the church bells ringing
All the world is singing
It's a brand new day.

The trees are full of blossom
The flowers are on their way.
God has made all these things
For all of us today.

John Michael Moore (8) St Hilda's Church, Hunts Cross, Liverpool.

May 2nd

Our Father, please send lots of sunshine so that Daddy can make silage and that Mammy can set her vegetables. Please help me to be good and help my family to go to church every Sunday to praise you and give you thanks.

David Heaslip (8) Kilmore School, Cavan.

May 3rd

Dear God, thank you for the stars and the moon and the sun and the plants and our solar system.

Ryan Oliver (7) St Nicholas' Church, Radford Semele, Warwickshire.

May 4th

Dear God, we thank you for animals that surround us, for trees and flowers, for birds that sing in the blue sky. We thank you for paper, coal and oil which come from nature. So thank you for nature and all living creatures. For Jesus' sake.

Benjamin Littley (7) Read C of E School, Burnley, Lancashire.

May 5th

Dear God, thank you for flowers and animals, and the food and rain for the plants. Thank you for thunder and lightning. Thank you for colours, purple, yellow, blue and green, red and orange, and brown and blond.

Charlotte McConnell (7) 8th Aughton Church Brownies, Ormskirk, Lancashire.

May 6th

Dear God, thank you for the living creatures. They are beautiful because they have colours and patterns.

Kate Hodgson (8) Bishop Goodwin Infant School, Carlisle, Cumbria.

May 7th
Dear Lord Jesus, thank you for the flowers down the road and in my garden.
Oliver Pash (5) The Seekers Group, St George's Church, Fovant, Wiltshire.

May 8th
Dear God, thank you for all the nice things in my town, and the people and cars. Thank you for looking after us.
Mark Wyre (7) St Stephen & All Martyrs Cubs, Great Lever, Lancashire.

May 9th
Dear God, thank you for all the different kinds of weather and the lovely green grass that me and my friends play on. Thank you for the lovely flowers that spring up everywhere, daffodils, tulips and daisies and many others. Thank you for all the little insects which you have made, like ladybirds and ants.
Emma Franckel (8) St Gabriel's C of E Primary School, Huyton, Merseyside.

May 10th
Dear God, thank you for the lovely countryside all around Britain. Thank you for hot countries around the world, and all the different countries from the cold North Pole to the hot Sahara desert.
Matthew Trickett (8) St Peter's C of E School, Pedmore, West Midlands.

May 11th
Dear God, thank you for making the world so beautiful.
James Hodgkinson (4) St Stephen's Sunday School, Norbury, London.

May 12th
Dear Lord Jesus, thank you for the lovely rain forests which animals live in; a tree frog sticking to a tree; a sloth hanging upside down; a big snake hissing up a tree, an anteater looking for ants on the floor; a little parrot flying. There are eagles in the rain forests too; and toucans, whose beaks are big and very bright.
Rachael Joynes (6) St Mary's C of E Infant School, Prestbury, Gloucestershire.

We ask God to help us to take care of it:

May 13th

Dear God, help us to take care of your world
and not to be tempted to ruin it. This is your world,
not just a part of it but all of it, so please don't
let us be selfish.

*Hayley Gilbert (9) Selwood Anglican/Methodist Middle School,
Frome, Somerset.*

> Christian Aid week usually takes place about now.
> 'Jesus said "whatever you did for anyone here
> you did for me"' Matthew 25:40

May 14th

Dear God, thank you that we have clean water
and food, and enough rain. In some countries they
have no clean water and hardly any food. In Christian
Aid Week help me to collect my spare pennies and
give them.

Kate Glover (5) Lightcliffe C of E School, Halifax, West Yorkshire.

> We thank God for all our food:

May 15th

Dear Lord, thank you for food. Thank you for the vitamins and fibre in food. We are sorry that we sometimes eat too much bad food. Please help us to eat the right amount of food each day, and the right kind of food each day.

Alex Bradshaw (8) Riseley C of E Lower School, Bedfordshire.

May 16th

Thank you God for the food we eat. Thank you God for the food we buy. Thank you God for the knives and forks and spoons we eat with.
Thank you God for everything.

Louise Berwick (9) St Kentigern's Sunday School, Aspatria, Cumbria.

May 17th

Dear God, bless me, my family and friends. Thank you for this day you have given us to have fun in our work and play. We thank you for the food you have given us and we hope tomorrow will be like today.

Martina Hegarty (8) New Mills, Letterkenny, Co. Donegal.

May 18th
Dear God, thank you for our food, especially fish and chips and choc ices. Please help the people who haven't got any food to get some so they don't die.
Andrew Brackett (5) Holy Trinity Church Club, Wednesfield Heath, West Midlands.

May 19th
Dear God, thank you for the hens that lay eggs and the sheep that give us wool, and thank you for the cows that give us milk.
Sara Dumbell (6) 4th St Ann's Rainbows, Rainhill, Merseyside.

and we thank God for things to drink:

May 20th
Dear God, thank you for drinks like lemonade, cola, orange juice, water, milk, tea and coffee. When we drink them we don't get thirsty.
Helen Martin (7) Matlock All Saints' Infants School, Matlock, Derbyshire.

About this time of the year it is Ascension Day, when Jesus went back to heaven.
> 'He was taken up to heaven as they watched him' Acts 1:9

May 21st

Thank you God for sending Jesus to help us to do right, not evil. Thank you Jesus for going to heaven so you could help everyone.

Ioan (8) Gemma (7) Edward (6) Helen (5) Orton C of E School, Penrith, Cumbria.

> We pray for those who don't have enough to keep them alive:

May 22nd

Dear Lord God, please help me as I worry about people who have no food or have nowhere to live and no clothes. I also worry about the violence and crime and unhappy people, the old and the sick. Please look after all these people. God bless everybody.

Samantha Osborne (9) 3rd Plumstead Common Brownies, Church of the Ascension, Plumstead, London.

May 23rd
Dear Father, thank you for the food and water you give us to survive. Sometimes I find myself so greedy when there is a huge plate of food in front of me, and I think of the people in the world who are starving. Please help the food of the world to be spread out evenly, not with some people starving and others with too much.
Adam White (8) Riseley C of E Lower School, Bedfordshire.

and we give thanks for people who help us:

May 24th
Dear God, thank you for the milkman who delivers the milk so we have milk to drink.
Kate Walker (5) Cinnamon Brow C of E School, Warrington, Cheshire.

May 25th
Thank you God for all the people you have given talents to, to create things for us. Those who catch fish for us to eat, bricklayers who build our houses, and for artists who give us colour in our homes, and for the earth you have made with all its beauty. Thank you God for everything.
Philip Wilburn (8) Goole, Humberside.

May 26th
Dear God, thank you for the countryside and for the houses we live in. Thank you for TV and radio. Thank you for people who can help us; policemen, doctors and firemen. Please help them in their work.

Andrew Holmes (8) St Peter's C of E School, Pedmore, West Midlands.

May 27th
Dear God, thank you for all the lighthouses and the foghorns so that ships can steer clear of the rocks.

Katie Smart (8) The Beacon Primary School, Exmouth, Devon.

May 28th
Dear God, thank you for my school, for my teacher who helps me to read and write, and for my friends.

Rachael France (5) St John the Baptist Church, Kirkheaton, Huddersfield, West Yorkshire.

May 29th

Dear God, thank you for our families and friends, for our schools, for books, pens and paper, and for our Sunday Schools where we learn the stories in the Bible. Thank you for sending Jesus to us so we may be saved.

Lynda Rawsthorn (8) St Mary's Adventurers Junior Sunday School, Walton-on-the-Hill, Southport, Merseyside.

May 30th

Thank you Lord for the Vicar, Curate and Lay Readers in the church. Thank you that they help to spread the message about you.

Rachel Rudman (9) St John's Explorers, Hensingham, Whitehaven, Cumbria.

> About this time of year we celebrate Pentecost, when God gave us the gift of the Holy Spirit.
>> 'When the day of Pentecost came, all the believers were gathered together in one place . . . They were all filled with the Holy Spirit.'
>> Acts 2:1 and 4

May 31st

O Lord my God, help me each day to learn about you, and help me to tell others about your love and how good you are. Bring peace and love to the world. Help those who are homeless and give strength to the weak and feed those with no food. Heal the sick, release your Holy Spirit on to the world and be with us always.

Colin James Parrett (8) St Lawrence Explorers, Kirkdale, Liverpool.

June brings tulips, lilies, roses,
Fills the children's hands with posies

Now summer has come and we can have fun outdoors.

'Let everything everywhere praise the Lord' *Psalm 103:22*

June 1st

Dear Lord, thank you for the sun so we can enjoy our days out. We can have picnics in the sun and play games. Thank you for the rain so our flowers and plants can grow. Thank you Lord for the sun and the rain.

Michelle Lorraine Smith (8) St Saviour's Sunday School, Bamber Bridge, Lancashire.

June 2nd

Dear God, thank you for all the sports, like football, cricket, cycle and motor car racing. Help us to keep our eyes sharp to see people who need our help and help us to keep our ears open to hear your call.

Mark Rayner (9) St John the Baptist Boys' Brigade, Ragworth, Cleveland.

June 3rd

Dear God, thank you for time to spend enjoying ourselves, playing football, going swimming and having parties. We thank you Lord for everything.

Shane Dawkins (9) Dewhurst St Mary C of E Primary School, Cheshunt, Hertfordshire.

June 4th
Dear God, the world is OK; thanks for the swings in the park, the swimming pools and skipping ropes and everything else.
Charlotte Stokoe (8) Battyeford C of E School, West Yorkshire.

June 5th
Dear God, thank you for my big bike.
Lee Cotterill (6) St Mary's & St Thomas' C of E Primary School, St Helens, Merseyside.

June 6th
Thank you God for my roller skates that Santa gave me at Christmas.
Caroline Tyson (5) Longview Primary School, Huyton, Merseyside.

June 7th
Thank you for letting us have fun Lord.
Kevin Abrahams (9) Dewhurst St Mary C of E Primary School, Cheshunt, Hertfordshire.

We ask God to help us to be good sports:

June 8th
Dear God, help everybody to be a good sport and not to boast. Help people to accept losing in races and to congratulate the winner of the race.
Andrew Tinker (8) Read C of E School, Burnley, Lancashire.

and to realize that we can't always have our own way:

June 9th
Dear God, help us to learn that we cannot have our own way all the time. Help us to learn that money cannot buy your love. Thank you for our lives and love, and help us to use our love to love other people.
Kathryn Brisland (7) Ipswich, Suffolk.

nor have everything we want:

June 10th
Dear God, help us to understand that we cannot get everything we want – like tractors and all sorts of things.
Philip Steadman (8) Ravenstonedale Endowed School, Ravenstonedale, Kirkby Stephen, Cumbria.

but sadly some people are bad and steal things:

June 11th
Dear Jesus, some people came into our house and took Daddy's tape player. Please Jesus, help these people to be good and not to go into people's houses.

Lizzy Burrows (4) St John the Baptist Church, Kirkheaton, Huddersfield, West Yorkshire.

It is a busy time at school:

June 12th
Thank you Lord for our school, which holds a lot of memories. Thank you for our school teachers who take care of us during school hours.

Christopher Cowell (9) St Aidan's C of E Primary School, Blackburn, Lancashire.

June 13th

Dear Lord, thank you for schools. Thank you for teachers who give up their time to help us to read and write. Thank you that we are able to come to school and learn things every day; sorry for all the wrong things we do at school. Please help us to be able to learn and work hard at everything we do. Please help the people who aren't able to go to school and learn.

Justine Cook (8) Riseley C of E Lower School, Bedfordshire.

June 14th

Dear God, please make me good at my work and please take care of me when I am playing with my friends. Help me to be good in assembly and please help me not to talk when my teacher is doing her work.

Dale Bartley (7) Longview Primary School, Huyton, Merseyside.

June 15th

Thank you God for our friends and relations. Thank you for our lovely schools that are so peaceful, and try to help the children in schools in other places that are not as fortunate as us.

Jacob Higgitt (8) St Peter's C of E School, Pedmore, West Midlands.

June 16th

Hello God! It's me. Please help me to be good in school, to get all my work finished, and most of all help me to be a kind friend to the other children in my class. Please God, bless everyone in my school, the teachers, the dinner ladies and all the children.

David Hughes (7) St Philip with St David Church, Liverpool.

We have to work hard to do tests and exams:

June 17th

Dear God, please help me because I never get 10 out of 10.

Jamie Walwyn (7) St Nicholas' Church, Radford Semele, Warwickshire.

June 18th

Our Father in heaven, I am sorry for the things I have done wrong. Please help me to do my spellings at school.

Craig Galley (7) St Stephen & All Martyrs Cubs, Great Lever, Lancashire.

and sometimes so do grown-ups:

June 19th

Dear God, help my mum in her exam about nursing because she is finding it a bit hard. Please help her. In your holy name.

Daniel Lawton (8) Padgate C of E Primary School, Warrington, Cheshire.

but we have a lot of fun together:

June 20th

Dear God, thank you for this school, for the lovely things we do here. May you be with us in song, game and story. Thank you for forgiving us when we have done wrong. Help us to learn. In Jesus' name.

Kimberly Mayren (8) St Mark's C of E School, Pemberton, Greater Manchester.

June 21st

Dear God, thank you for my friends. Thank you for letting me go to school.

Jon Bradshaw (6) Witney Parish Church Sunday Schools, Oxfordshire.

June 22nd
Please God, help us to have a nice day today in the playground. Thank you God.

Anthony Jones (6) Longview CP School, Huyton, Merseyside.

June 23rd
Dear God, thank you for friends to play with in the playground, and for families that love and care for me. Please help me to care for everybody as well as they do for me.

Juliet Tanti (7) Read C of E School, Burnley, Lancashire.

June 24th
Dear God, thank you for school trips. I pray nobody falls over or traps their fingers in the door. I pray everybody has a lovely time and is good.

Harry Ferdinando (6) Riseley C of E Lower School, Bedfordshire.

but life at school isn't always easy:

June 25th
Dear God, I don't always like school but I have to go to get an education. People shout and make a noise and I get headaches. Please help me to like school and help people to be a little bit quieter.

Sarah Lynch (8) St Laurence Junior Church, Ramsgate, Kent.

so we are grateful for good friends:
> 'Kind words are like honey, sweet and good for you' Proverbs 16:24

June 26th
Thank you for my friends and for my time at play.
Bless little children everywhere, dear Lord, I pray.
Clare Livingstone (4) Derrygortreavy, Benburb, Armagh.

although sometimes we fall out with them:

June 27th
Dear God, thank you for friends and friendship
so that we can talk and play together. I'm sorry for
all the times when I have fallen out with my friends.
Please help me to make more friends with people
who are lonely, and help me to make friends again
when I have fallen out with my friends.
Hannah Botterill (8) Riseley C of E Lower School, Bedfordshire.

June 28th
Dear God, the boy across the street will not make
friends. Will you help me please?
Paul Halliwell (9) Christ Church Boys' Brigade, Walton Breck, Liverpool.

but Jesus is always there for us:
> 'Remember, I will be with you always, even until the end of time' Matthew 28:20

June 29th
Dear Jesus, thank you for being a fisher of men. Thank you for being our shepherd. Thank you for being our Lord.
Callum Brown (8) St James' Junior Church, Morpeth, Northumberland.

and God is always our friend:

June 30th
Dear Father God, you are our friend. You are with us always. You forgive us if we are naughty and say sorry. You love us always. We love you. Thank you for everything.
Kim Hartshorne (3) St James' Sunday School, Chapelthorpe, West Yorkshire.

Hot *July* brings cooling showers,
Apricots and gillyflowers

Today we start the second half of the year.

July 1st
Dear Lord, we appreciate the days of the week and the Anglo-Saxons who named them. Thank you for all you have created. Thank you for Sunday, my special day because my dad is home all day.
Thomas White (7) St Peter's School, Pedmore, West Midlands.

and we have a lot to thank God for:

July 2nd
Dear Lord, thank you for our world and everything in it. The trees that stand in the sun and the birds that sing in the trees. Thank you for our food and drink, and help us to make this world a better place for us all.
Helen Renshaw (8) St Maxentius Sunday School, Bradshaw, Lancashire.

July 3rd
Thank you God for loving my family and giving us food and shelter in your beautiful world.
Daisy Swain (8) The School House, Hartfield, East Sussex.

July 4th

Dear God, thank you for the living things; birds that sing, bright coloured flowers and trees. Thank you God for animals, from a little beetle to the big giraffe. God made people; little or big, thin or fat, poor or rich, bad or good. Thank you God for them all.

Christopher Wheatley (7) Ravenstonedale Endowed School, Cumbria.

July 5th

Thank you Lord for the colours
Thank you Lord for flowers and bees
Thank you Lord for birds and trees
Thank you Lord for lovely food
Thank you Lord for people
Thank you Lord for school and work
Thank you Lord for everything

Gemma Lawton (8) Wantage C of E Infants' School, Oxfordshire.

July 6th

Dear Lord, thank you for our senses. Thank you that we can smell the scented flowers. We love to hear the birds singing in the tall trees and the waves crashing against the rocks. We love the sweet taste of juicy oranges and the delicious taste of newly boiled potatoes with melted butter. And to feel the softness of my new rabbit.

Kirstin McKay (9) St Bartholomew's Church, Gourock, Renfrewshire.

July 7th

Dear Lord, thank you for the food we share, vegetables and fruit, meat and bread. Please help the people in third world countries so they can live happily.

Oliver Brandwood (9) Gosforth C of E School, Gosforth, Seascale, Cumbria.

July 8th

Dear Lord our Father, thank you for everything: For being there for us, for the world we live in with our families and friends. For things to do, for our animals and pets. Thank you that when we are ill there are hospitals, doctors and nurses to look after us. Thank you for giving us Jesus, for the Lord's Prayer and your Church. We pray that people will love each other more and know your peace.

The Haylos Group (ages 7–9) St Nicholas Church, Charlwood, Surrey.

July 9th

We love you Jesus. Thank you for all you give us. Thank you for food and flowers and mummies and daddies and grannies and grandads, and birds and elephants and for snakes too. Alleluia! And we must remember to thank you for food before we eat.

Christ Church Junior Church nursery class, Nailsea, Bristol, Avon.

July 10th

Thank you God, for all you have done for us.
Thank you for trees and cars.
Thank you for being kind and for making us kind.
Thank you for our homes and our families.
Thank you for our eyes, ears and legs.
Thank you for everything.

Katie Leonard, Joanne Rochell, Stephanie King, Charlotte Atkinson (all aged 6), Christ the King, Battyeford, West Yorkshire.

July 11th

Dear God, thank you for the world. It was so good of you to think of it, and make all the people and me and all our houses. Thank you for everything.

Amy Hyde (6) St John's Church, Kenilworth, Warwickshire.

July 12th

Thank you God for sun and rain and fields and the countryside, and for houses, flats and bungalows, and lots of other things.

Gemma Foran (9) 20th Liverpool Brownies, Merseyside.

July 13th
Dear Lord, thank you for the sun. It helps the plants grow, it is hot, and most people like the sun.
Emma Louise Lawson (7) St Saviour's Sunday School, Bamber Bridge, Lancashire.

July 14th
Dear God, thank you for water and life and me.
John Pearce (6) Lilliput First VC School, Poole, Dorset.

A big thank-you:

July 15th
Thank you for the things we do, the parks, the rivers
   and wildlife too.
For all these things we thank you.
Thank you for the things to do, for tennis clubs, youth
   club and cubs, brownies, rainbows too.
For all these things we thank you.
Our village has a lovely school. It also has a
   swimming pool.
For all these things we thank you.
We have a lovely church and vicar. At Christmas there
   is an angel made of wicker.
For all these things we thank you.
Nice helpful people and friends surround us and lend
   a hand without a fuss.

For all these things we thank you.
For my mum and dad, brother and grandparents too,
   my home, and Lord I love you.
For all these things we thank you Lord.
Angela Greaves (6) St Mary the Virgin, Ketton, Lincolnshire.

And a thank you from a visitor from another country:

July 16th
Dear Lord, thank you for the love you give us every day and for the lovely time I'm spending in England. Thank you for the lovely school I'm going to. Give food to the ones who haven't got anything, and help the countries that are at war.
Etienne Diganeau (9) St Nicholas Church, Radford Semele, Warwickshire.

And thank you prayers for our homes, our friends and possessions:

July 17th
Dear God, we thank you for our houses to keep warm in, our pets or teddies to comfort us, our churches to pray and think in, and our family and friends.
Nicola Thwaite (9) St Mary's Sunday School, Wigton, Cumbria.

July 18th
Thank you God for my computer.
Henry Wagner (3) St Paul's Sunday School, Honiton, Devon.

> Some children don't have much food or clothing to keep them warm and healthy, or any toys or treats to enjoy:

July 19th
Dear Lord Jesus, we have lots of shops near here where we go to buy all the things we need to keep us healthy, warm and well-fed. Thank you for them. We have lots of shops where we go to buy our treats: toys, sweets and presents. Thank you for them, too. We are lucky to have treats, and we think of all the children in poorer countries who have to spend all day finding water and food just to survive, and they never have any money for treats. Please look after them.
Witney Parish Church Sunday Schools, Oxfordshire.

July 20th

Dear Father, do not just help us but help other people in poorer countries, so that they get enough food and drink. Please stop all this horrid fighting and bombing. Just let us stop and think for a moment of all those people who have been injured or killed.

James Merrick (8) St Peter's C of E School, Pedmore, West Midlands.

July 21st

Dear Jesus, thank you for our clothes and food. Help the boys and girls who are sick and have no food. Help me to be a good girl too.

Jennifer Maubury (5) Annaghmore Parish Sunday School, Co. Armagh.

July 22nd

Every day O Lord I pray
For those children far away
So short of food and clothes and love.
Please Lord from your throne above
Send peace to them and mercy mild
For each and every little child.

Hayley Walker (8) St Thomas the Martyr C of E School, Upholland, Lancashire.

July 23rd
Dear God, we are all very thankful for all you have given us. Please help those who are blind and those who are in hospital today.
Elisabeth Kerton (9) Cirencester Parish Church F.O.G. Club, Gloucestershire.

Hooray! Holiday time is coming:

July 24th
Dear God, thank you for holidays. They are fun. Thank you for the sun and the sea and the sand which we enjoy. Thank you for the countryside we can explore.
Daniel Campbell (7) Read C of E School, Burnley, Lancashire.

July 25th
Dear God, we pray for mums and dads, grandmas, grandads, aunties and uncles, for sunshine and for safe journeys on holiday.
St Gregory's Sunday School (ages 3–8) Goodleigh, North Devon.

We enjoy outings:

July 26th

Dear God, I am going on a Beaver outing today. Please keep us safe on the bus and help us to be good Beavers. Bless my family.

Sara Nairn (6) Letterkenny, Co. Donegal.

and doing things with our friends:

July 27th

Dear God, thank you for our world. Thank you for Rainbows, Brownies, Guides, Rangers, Cubs and Scouts. Thank you for letting us work and learn. Thank you for friendship.

Jenna Beardsworth (8) St Christopher's Church 47th Blackpool Brownies, Marton, Lancashire.

July 28th

Dear Lord, thank you for our food and fresh water. Thank you for families and friends. Thank you for Brownies and Guides. Thank you for churches, and for Jesus and God looking after us.

Diana Johnson (9) Charlotte Raynor (7) 1st Muskham Brownies, Newark, Nottinghamshire.

We have special days:

July 29th
Dear God, thank you for special days such as our birthdays. Thank you also for special days when we have celebrations but especially for holidays.
Michael Graham (7) St Peter's School, Pedmore, West Midlands.

   and parties:

July 30th
Thank you God for birthdays. Thank you for my friends. Thank you for the cakes and cards and the presents people send.
Gregory Osbourn (7) 13th St Mary's Beavers, Far Cotton, Northampton.

July 31st
Thank you Jesus for my birthday and party. We all had a lovely time at my party. We played lots of nice games and ate nice food. Thank you for my presents.
Charlotte McIlroy (5) St Paul's Sunday School, Starcross, Exeter, Devon.

August brings the sheaves of corn, Then the harvest home is borne

We have fun with our families and friends.

August 1st

Thank you God for making my family like the
sun, which shines brightly and makes me warm.
I feel cosy when they are around me. Thank you for
my parents. They love me and look after me, and for
my sisters who I play with. I am very sorry for all the
wrong things I've done to hurt them and make them
feel sad. I love my family more than anything. I thank
you for giving them to me. Please help them if they
are ever in trouble, as they help me. Thank you
for my family.

Lynn Beattie (8) Monasteroris National School, Edenderry, Co. Offaly.

August 2nd

Dear God, my sister is lovely, my cat called Thomas
purrs a lot, Mummy makes us delicious cakes, Daddy
plays football with me. I love my family very much.
Thank you dear good God for loving us.

Abbie Dorey (8) Valence Road, Lewes, East Sussex.

August 3rd

Thank you God for Mummy and Daddy, my
family and my friends. Thank you God for making
a beautiful world. Thank you God for Jesus and all
the things that make me happy.

Sarah Wood (7) Bilsdale, North Yorkshire.

August 4th
Thank you God for
>   my F amily
>   being A ltogether
>   my M ammy and Daddy
>   I nviting my friends to play
>   I L ove
>   Y ou

Elizabeth Daniels (6) New Ross, Co. Wexford.

August 5th
Dear God, I like ice cream but I love my family.
Richard Gordon (5) Bangor Parish, Co. Down.

August 6th
Dear Father God, help all the families all over the world. Look after them when working, playing, eating, drinking and sleeping. Be our friend for ever and ever.
Brian Handcock (8) Camross, Mountrath, Co. Laoise.

and especially our dads and mums:

August 7th
Dear God, I thank you for my mother because she always kisses me at bedtime and when I am unwell she looks after me. I thank you for my father because he is a happy man and he is nice to me.
Lili Sharman (8) West Chiltington C of E School, Pulborough, West Sussex.

and grans:

August 8th
Thank you Lord for my Nannie and for my two brothers who make my breakfast on my birthday.
Rachel Way (5) St George's J Team, Chichester, West Sussex.

and grandads:

August 9th
Thank you God for my kind Grandad. He loves me and gives me sweets.
Michael Sutherland (4) Longview Primary School, Huyton, Merseyside.

as well as brothers and sisters:

August 10th
Thank you God for mums and dads and granddads and grandmas. Thank you for me, but most of all thank you for my baby brother.
Claire Hunter (6) St Francis' Church, Kitt Green, Wigan, Lancashire.

August 11th
Thank you God for my sister. When I fall over she puts a plaster on my knee.
Graeme Hilton (5) St Thomas C of E Primary School, Lydiate, Merseyside.

August 12th
Thank you God for my brother. He looks after me. He does my breakfast.
Toni Becker (6) St Thomas C of E Primary School, Lydiate, Merseyside.

August 13th
Thank you God for my sister. We play crocodiles and sometimes she bites my finger because she is only a baby.
Jessica Dunn (5) St Thomas C of E Primary School, Lydiate, Merseyside.

We enjoy playing with our friends:

August 14th
Dear God, friendship is caring; friendship is sharing; friendship is helping; friendship is telling each other secrets.
Alice Boardman (5) St Mary's & St Thomas' C of E Primary School, St Helens, Merseyside.

August 15th
Dear God, thank you for all my friends and all the good times we have playing together in the holidays.
Katharine Lister (9) St Saviour's Sunday School, Raynes Park, London.

August 16th
Dear Lord, I thank you for chocolate, toys, swimming pools, sunshine, sand and trains.
Gregory Young (3) St James' Junior Church, Morpeth, Northumberland.

August 17th
Dear Jesus, thank you for the slide in the park.
Stephen Berry (5) Newburgh C of E School, Lancashire.

August 18th
Thank you Lord for giving us cartoons and entertainment.
Matthew Stones (9) St Stephen & All Martyrs Cubs, Great Lever, Lancashire.

August 19th
Dear Heavenly Father, we thank you for letting us have all the sports we have and giving us good health.
John Wilson (9) Holy Trinity Episcopal Church, Kilmarnock, Ayrshire.

August 20th
Dear Jesus, thank you for trains and for my toys.
Garreth Pennington (4) Newburgh C of E School, Lancashire.

August 21st
Dear God, thank you for cars, because we can go a long way in them.
Gavin Craig (7) St Mary's Church, Marshalswick, Hertfordshire.

August 22nd
Dear God, you are good at cars.
Darren Wells-Burr (6) St John's Seekers, Tatworth, Somerset.

and we enjoy being at home during the day:

August 23rd
Thank you God for good food and cosy beds and toys to play with in our homes, bikes to ride on and shoes to wear.
Andrew Fields (7) Moy Parish Church Sunday School, Co. Tyrone.

and at bedtime:

August 24th
Dear God, thank you for our teddies. Thank you for shelves to put them on and beds to share.
Jamie Taylor (5) Orton C of E School, Penrith, Cumbria.

August 25th
Dear God, thank you for bedtime stories and nice warm beds. Thank you for families that live together and I hope they will for ever. Thank you Lord.
Jacqui Raine (8) Ravenstonedale Endowed School, Ravenstonedale, Kirkby Stephen, Cumbria.

when we say our prayers:

August 26th
Hello God, it's me. I want to say thank you for providing me with clothes and lots of other good things, and for your love and kindness. I pray to you every night. Thank you for the sunshine and the beauty of the world.

Annmarie Blundell (9) St Peter's School, Formby, Merseyside.

Sometimes we have bad dreams or nightmares:

August 27th
Dear God, please stop us having nightmares and deliver us from evil; sorry for being naughty. Please take care of all our friends and family.

Laura Hobbs (6) Uccle School, Brussels, Belgium.

and we ask God to look after us:

August 28th
Lord of all the angels bright
Guard me while I sleep tonight
Angels' wings around me spread
Keep me safe till morning light.

Alexander and Richard Pattenden (4) Thames Ditton, Surrey.

Harvesting is taking place:

August 29th
Dear God, harvest has come. Tomatoes to pick, barley safe in bags, apples just ripe, carrots and potatoes ready in boxes, waiting for a lorry to take them to the shops. Tractors in fields, combine harvesters working. Harvest is here; thank you.
Laura Morgan (9) Selwood Anglican/Methodist Middle School, Frome, Somerset.

August 30th
Dear God, thank you for making the people who go to fetch the food we eat. The fishermen who go on dangerous journeys to get the fish that we eat. We thank you for farmers who grow crops that the sun and rain have helped to grow, and for the animals they keep, the cows who provide milk which makes all sorts of things, and pigs and lambs. We thank you Lord God for all these things.
Emma Nash (9) St Stephen's C of E School, Whelley, Wigan, Lancashire.

August 31st
Dear God, the world is lovely. I'm glad that you made the world.
Jonathan Michael Smith (7) Christ the King, Battyeford, West Yorkshire.

Warm *September* brings the fruit, Sportsmen then begin to shoot

We thank God for his wonderful world.
'O Lord, you are worthy to receive the glory
and the honour and the power, for you have
created all things' *Revelation 4:11*

September 1st
Dear God For Springtime
>Sun
>Summer
and Harvesting
of Jesu's love we sing

>For Autumn
>>Wind
>>Winter
>and Christmas carolling
>our praise we bring.

Christopher Smith (8) Hapton Methodist Church, Burnley, Lancashire.

September 2nd
Dear Lord, thank you for the trees and the flowers of the world, and all the animals, birds and insects of the world. Help us Lord to look after all of these things.

Helen Hughes (8) St Margaret's Church, Burnage, Manchester.

September 3rd
Dear Father in Heaven, I know I am very lucky to live in the country where I can always see animals, birds and flowers. I pray for all those children who are not as lucky as I am. Dear Father, please bless, protect and care for all the children in the world.
Sarah Orridge (7) Eythorne Benefice, Shepherdswell, Dover, Kent.

September 4th
Dear God, thank you for all the animals you have made. Thank you for the plants that grow, thank you for the rain and sun. I know that you are watching me all the time and I know that you love me always.
Sarah Forbes (7) St Anne's Church, Copp, Preston, Lancashire.

September 5th
Dear God, thank you for the sun, and the dogs and the rabbits and the ducks and the insects.
Hannah McCulloch (6) St Wulfram's Sunday School, Grantham, Lincolnshire.

and also for ourselves and for our bodies:
'Everything that can breathe, praise the Lord'
Psalm 150:6

September 6th

Dear Father God, thank you for life and everything that has life; the birds and plants and the things that keep us alive. Lord, thank you for the trees that give us oxygen and fruit. Thank you for our bodies and blood and lungs and heart.

Deborah Lamb (8) St Mary's Sunday School, Old Hall, Warrington, Cheshire.

September 7th

Dear God, thank you for making us able to run about and talk and use our arms and legs properly. Let us take care of people less fortunate than ourselves.

Steven Heard (8) St Peter's C of E School, Pedmore, West Midlands.

> As we go back to school:
> 'Choose knowledge rather than the finest gold'
> Proverbs 8:10

September 8th

Dear Lord, thank you very much for our teachers. If we did not have teachers we would not have a good education. Please help me to do my school work properly and then the teacher will be pleased with me. Please help all the children in the world to have a good education so that they can help others.

Michelle Young (9) Gomersal Middle School, West Yorkshire.

September 9th

Dear God, thank you for helping me to learn my work. Help me to play without fighting with my friends, because I care about them like you care about us.

Danielle Hamilton (7) Longview Primary School, Huyton, Merseyside.

September 10th

Dear Jesus, please help us to be kind and if someone is feeling sad say 'come and play with me' so then they will be happy.

Nicola Michelle Tracey (6) St Stephen's C of E School, Whelley, Lancashire.

September 11th
Thank you God for paper and pencils and pens to write with. Thank you God for rulers and colours and lights. God, you are so nice, you help people.
Oliver Crarer (7) Matlock All Saints' Infants School, Matlock, Derbyshire.

September 12th
Dear God, thank you for helping me and making me better. Help me to do my work in school and thank you for my friends.
Douglas McKenzie (5) Moy Parish Church Sunday School, Co. Tyrone.

> God's love is always there.
>> 'God showed how much he loved us by sending his only Son into this world' 1 John 4:9

September 13th
Dear Lord, thank you for my life, my mother who is always there to help put things right, my father who guides me on the right path, my brothers who play with me and always make me laugh. But when bad things happen, God, you are always there to hear my prayer. At the close of day, when all are asleep, I pray you Lord my soul to keep.
Christopher Turton (8) St Mary's Church, Prescot, Merseyside.

September 14th
Our Father, we love you, and help us to be good.
Jonathon Robinson (7) St John the Baptist Boys' Brigade, Ragworth, Cleveland.

September 15th
Dear Jesus, you made me. I love you.
Susannah Thompson (3) St Francis of Assisi Church, Wigan, Lancashire.

September 16th
Dear Lord, we love you and you know we do; and you love us, even if we sometimes don't feel it.
Emlyn Robbins (8) Moordown St John's Sunday School, Bournemouth, Dorset.

> 'Dear friends, let us love one another, for love comes from God' 1 John 4:7

September 17th
Dear God, I think people should spread love around.
Thomas Naughton (6) St Luke's Church, Lowton, Cheshire.

At our harvest festivals we thank God for all he has given us and remember those who do not have enough.

'When you are reaping at harvest, if you forget a sheaf do not go back and get it. Leave it for the foreigners, the orphans and the widows.'
Deuteronomy 24:19

September 18th

Dear God, Harvest is fields of golden crops,
Harvest is wheat, barley, oats and maize,
Harvest is combines crunching through corn,
Harvest is trailers loaded with grain.

Harvest is bulging trees with ripening fruit,
Harvest is golden and brown, russet and bronze,
Harvest is potatoes, cauliflowers, cabbages and carrots,
Harvest is having enough to eat.

Harvest is churches filled with fruit and flowers,
Harvest is autumn piled on window sills,
Harvest is 'We plough the fields and scatter',
Harvest is saying thank you to God for all he provides.

Harvest is stony fields parched and dry,
Harvest is dried up streams and rivers,
Harvest is sparse crops, weak and
   withered,
Harvest is empty grain stores.

Harvest is disease and misery in poor
   countries,
Harvest is hungry children, empty
   stomachs,
Harvest is praying to God for help,
Harvest is too little.

Children from St Oswald's Church, Brereton, Cheshire.

September 19th
Dear Lord, thank you for the food you give us. Thank you for the flowers that give us seeds. Thank you for the machines that plough the fields. Thank you for people who repair the machines that go wrong.

Simon Craven (9) St Mary the Virgin Junior Church, Docking, Norfolk.

September 20th
Dear Lord, thank you for the sunshine, the wind and the rain, and for making our gardens green again.

Stacey Douglas (7) 20th Liverpool Brownies, All Saints' Church, Childwall, Liverpool.

September 21st

Thank you Lord for the sun and rain
Thank you for the moon and stars
Thank you for the flowers and trees
Thank you Lord for the honeybees.
Thank you Lord for the animals we see,
Thank you for my brother and me,
Thank you Lord for my family.
Thank you Lord for the world we live in,
Thank you for the Church we sing in.
Thank you Lord for everything.

Diana Cherry (8) Christ Church Sunday School, Penrith, Cumbria.

September 22nd

H arvest is a time of work
A time of food
R ipe fruit and fresh vegetables
V ery happy time of the year
E ggs, wheat, corn and hay
S unny days to ripen fruit
T omatoes red and ripe.
      Thank you God.

Lee Angel (9) Selwood Anglican/Methodist Middle School, Frome, Somerset.

September 23rd
Thank you God for clothes to wear. Thank you God for giving us food.
Poppy Duffree (5) Harlaxton Sunday School, Grantham, Lincolnshire.

September 24th
Dear God, thank you for the trees which keep me cool when I am hot. Thank you for the sun which warms me. Thank you for the flowers which make me happy when I am sad. Thank you for good things to eat when I am hungry.
Leigh Slater (7) Read C of E School, Burnley, Lancashire.

September 25th
Dear God, thank you for all your gifts, and for good things like all the plants and creatures. Thank you for animals and people and the world, and my teachers and friends. Thank you God for always being my friend and helping me now through Jesus Christ.
Adam Hesketh (7) St David's Church, Haigh, Wigan, Lancashire.

We think of those who are not as fortunate as we are
   'If there are any among you who are poor, do not be selfish and refuse to help them'
   Deuteronomy 15:7

September 26th

Thank you
Lord for
all the
things you have given us
like grass and trees.
Please
help
others
that
are not
as lucky
as us.

Oliver Quinn (7) St Thomas' Mustard Seeds Junior Church, Thurstonland, West Yorkshire.

September 27th

Dear God, please help all the poor people to grow wheat and food and stop them starving.

Philip Harding (6) St Gabriel's C of E School, Huyton, Merseyside.

September 28th

Dear Lord, please help people who have got no shelter and who are hungry and thirsty and have nowhere to sleep tonight, whilst I snuggle up in a nice comfy bed. Please give them food and drink and somewhere to sleep.

Lauren Stevenson (8) St Gabriel's C of E School, Huyton, Merseyside.

September 29th

Dear Lord Jesus, please look after old and lonely people, and help children and grown-ups who have no food and no money. And please help women and men who can't get along with each other and have broken up.

Leanne Oldham (9) St Nicholas Church, Radford Semele, Warwickshire.

And to end the month of September, a thank you by a farmer's son:

September 30th

Dear God, thank you for lambs and sheep, tractors and cows, people, pots and bags and cats. Thank you for water and books, school and teddies, pigs, animals and farms.

Stuart Nelson (7) Orton C of E School, Penrith, Cumbria.

Fresh *October* brings the pheasant,
Then to gather nuts is pleasant

We thank God for all the different seasons.
'God chooses the right time for everything in the world'
Ecclesiastes 3:1

October 1st
Dear God, the thing I like best about Spring is playing in the fields; Summer the sunny days; Autumn jumping in the leaves, and last of all Winter throwing snowballs at my friends. Thank you God.
Kayleigh Phillips (8) Read C of E School, Burnley, Lancashire.

  and for creatures great and small:
    'God used soil from the ground to make all the animals and birds' Genesis 2:19

October 2nd
Dear God, please help us not to destroy your wonderful world by dropping litter, and in the rain forest not to chop down trees where animals are living happily. Please help us not to pollute rivers and the air. Thank you God for birds and fishes, and for loving families who care when you get hurt and teased.
Lois Wall (7) St Mary's C of E Infant School, Prestbury, Gloucestershire.

October 3rd

Dear God, thank you for all the creatures. I like it when the bees make honey and the spider spins a cobweb; in the morning the cobwebs are like silk. Without the creatures the world would be dull, so we won't kill the creatures.

Ashley Aitken (7) Bishop Goodwin Infant School, Carlisle, Cumbria.

October 4th

Dear God, thank you for giving the whale the big sea to swim in.

James Millar (5) St Peter's Sunday School, Weedon Bec, Northampton.

October 5th

Lord Jesus, the world that you made is wonderful. I especially like your animals. My favourite animal is the bear; I like its big nose and all its fluffy, woolly fur, and I like the way it moves, slowly plodding along. Thank you for all your creatures.

John Brackett (9) Holy Trinity Church Club, Wednesfield Heath, West Midlands.

October 6th
Dear God, please help snakes because they get killed for their skins, which get used for handbags and shoes.
Lewis Williams (8) Christ Church Boys' Brigade, Liverpool.

October 7th
Thank you God for all the animals of the world which give us pleasure, especially the house-trained animals. Please help the wild animals which some people want to kill. Also please help the rare species from being wiped out completely.
Helen Armstrong (8) Aghadowey Parish Sunday School, Coleraine.

October 8th
Dear Lord, thank you for the animals who keep us company. Thank you for the animals on the farms who feed us. We especially thank you for food, and for our families and friends.
Beth Gardner (7) St Peter's Church, Simonstone, Lancashire.

We give especial thanks for our pets:

October 9th

Dear Father, thank you for all the things you give us, for our families and friends, and for our pets.

Anna McAlpine (8) Holy Trinity Episcopal Church, Kilmarnock, Ayrshire.

October 10th

Thank you God for pets like dogs with nice fluffy fur, cats that can jump high distances, hamsters small, cute and furry, rabbits that hop around, squirrels that run up and down trees, and for all nature.

Dominic Sedgwick (8) Read C of E School, Burnley, Lancashire.

October 11th

Dear God, thank you for all the animals on the earth and in the sea, and thank you for my guinea pig.

Elizabeth Golney (7) Matlock All Saints' Infants School, Matlock, Derbyshire.

October 12th

Dear God, I love you and Mummy and Dad and my rabbit and hamster and goldfish.

Emma Mills (6) Mirfield Junior Church, West Yorkshire.

October 13th
Dear Jesus, thank you for mice, bats and tortoises.
Mark Parry (5) Newburgh C of E School, Lancashire.

October 14th
Dear God, thank you for the horse's legs so strong, to gallop across the green field. Thank you for his stable, warm, fresh and cosy. Thank you for his food, for oats, chaff and nuts.
Charlene Wade (8) St John's C of E Primary School, Enfield, Middlesex.

October 15th
Thank you God for Australian tree frogs, for Syrian, golden and dwarf hamsters, and for aquarium animals.
Samantha Mudd (5) Morpeth Parish Church, Northumberland.

October 16th
Dear God, I wish I had a mouse because they are cosy and cuddly.
Ruth Hartwell, Bishop Loveday School, Bodicote, Oxfordshire.

and ask God to help us care for them properly:
'Good people take care of their animals'
Proverbs 12:10

October 17th
Dear God, please help us not to be rough with any animals, and to give them water and food to let them live. Help us not to forget to feed them and not to forget to take them out to get some exercise to keep them healthy.
Terri Thompson (7) Longview Primary School, Huyton, Merseyside.

   especially when they are not well:

October 18th
Dear God, thank you for pets that keep us company when we are lonely. When they are sick help us to look after them properly, and please help Vets to make them better.
Nicola Clews (8) St Nicholas' Church, Radford Semele, Warwickshire.

October 19th
Dear Jesus, thank you for my dog. He is not very well. Please look after him.
Amy Milner (5) Newburgh C of E School, Lancashire.

October 20th
Dear God, please look after all the animals, the mammals and the fish. Please look after my pet rabbit and let it be all right.
Daniel Peter Clarke (7) St Stephen's C of E School, Whelley, Lancashire.

October 21st
Dear Lord our lovable Father. Please help our cat to get better, he is very ill and sick and old. He is 12 years old and has got cat leukaemia. Let him live some more years please.
Christopher Barkwill (8) St Peter & St James Church, Halwill, Beaworthy, Devon.

Sometimes things go wrong:

October 22nd
Dear Father God, please help me stop thinking about my hamster, as she ran away because we left her outside.
Gabriella Piper (7) Woodretts School, Worksop, Nottinghamshire.

October 23rd
Dear God, my nan has got a new dog but he hates cats. He nearly hurt our cat, so please could you make him like cats.
Sarah Campbell (8) St Michael's C of E Primary School, Enfield, Middlesex.

   and we are sad when they die:

October 24th
Dear Father God, on Sunday night my brother's terrapin died. My dad buried it today. My brother was sad because it was his terrapin. Thank you for the wonderful time we had with his terrapin.
Sarah Corrigan (7) St John the Baptist Church Brownies, Upperby, Cumbria.

October 25th
Dear God, our hamster has died. We are sad. Please take care of 'Hammy' and make us happy. We love you.
Iona Hamilton (4) North Street, Lewes, East Sussex.

October 26th
Please God, look after my mouse. I hope she will be happy with you and she won't be poorly in heaven.
Sam Carter (8) St Thomas' Mustard Seeds Junior Church, Thurstonland, West Yorkshire.

or are ill-treated:

October 27th
Dear God, thank you for our families and friends, and for trees and plants. I love horses but I don't like people who hurt animals, they are nasty. Please stop them and make them nice people.
Hayley Francis (8) St Laurence Junior Church, Ramsgate, Kent.

And help us always to be grateful for what we have:

October 28th
Dear Father, thank you for living creatures because they are important.
Anthony Stirzaker (7) Bishop Goodwin Infant School, Carlisle, Cumbria.

October 29th

Dear God, thank you for love and care of animals and people. Thank you for our pets and for Vets who look after them. You love everything, even predators.

William Coyne (7) Bishop Loveday School, Bodicote, Oxfordshire.

October 30th

Dear God, please help us to be grateful for what we have got. Help us to throw rubbish in bins, to work hard in school, to be nice and kind, to take care of animals, to take care of people, and to have fun.

Amy Bentley (8) Holy Spirit Church, Dovecot, Merseyside.

October 31st

Dear God, Thank you for the dogs that bark.
Thank you for the cats that miaow.
Thank you for the cows that moo.
Thank you for my family.
Thank you for school.
Thank you for my house.
Thank you for sweets and food.
Thank you for my toys.
Thank you for my bike.
Thank you for the trees.
Thank you for the plants that grow.
Thank you for the world.

Nicholas McQueen (6) Lightcliffe C of E School, Halifax, West Yorkshire.

Dull *November* brings the blast, Then the leaves are whirling fast

Jesus is King of everything and
everybody in heaven and on earth.
'He is Lord of Lords and King of Kings' *Revelation 17:14*

November 1st
Dear Jesus, I believe in you. I am friends with you. Will you be my King?
Christopher Archer (7) Crosby Ravensworth School, Cumbria.

November 2nd
Dear Jesus, thank you for all the lovely things you have done.
Francis Mountjoy (5) St John's Seekers, Tatworth, Somerset.

November 3rd
Jesus, you are my best friend. Thank you for our food and all the things you do for me.
Heather Maubury (4) Annaghmore Parish Sunday School, Co. Armagh.

'Jesus is always praying for us' Hebrews 7:25

November 4th
Dear Jesus, thank you for helping us to pray.
Poppy Bowdler (5) St Paul's Sunday School, Starcross, Exeter, Devon.

November 5th
My Lord you are powerful and clever. I love you so much I say my prayers at night and you listen to me. You greet me in the morning but it is not just me you love. You love the birds and the flowers and you love us all. You help when everything goes wrong and love the bad and good. Thank you. In Jesus' name.

Daniel Park (8) Ravenstonedale Endowed School, Ravenstonedale, Kirkby Stephen, Cumbria.

> So we pray for peace where there is war.
> 'Let the peace of Christ rule in your hearts'
> Colossians 3:15

November 6th
Dear Lord, I thank you for your world. Help me to understand what you are saying to me. Help the wars stop in the world; let peace come to all of us.

Daniel Czaicki (8) Riseley C of E Lower School, Bedfordshire.

November 7th
Lord Jesus, please help the children in lots of countries. Many often starve; they are poor, sometimes they are killed because of the wars. I love you, so do these children. Please help them.

Laura Dodd (7) Padgate C of E Primary School, Warrington, Cheshire.

November 8th

Dear God, I pray for the poor people and all those who are dying. Please help the children whose countries are at war, and I hope that one day there will be peace in our world. Thank you God.

Anthony James Byrne (6) St Thomas the Martyr, Upholland, Lancashire.

November 9th

Dear God, help people to believe in peace not war, and be kind and gentle. Help people to praise you. Make people be friendly to others, stop people suffering, and make people healthy so they may live and not die.

Beverley Louise Guy (9) Ravenstonedale Endowed School, Ravenstonedale, Kirkby Stephen, Cumbria.

November 10th

Please God, help me to look after others in the way they would look after me. Help the people who suffer wounds in battle. Help people to stop all wars, and help people to be brave when people from their family have died.

Helen Gibson (9) St Peter's School, Formby, Merseyside.

November 11th
Dear Father, we thank you for the children and grown-ups that died for us in the war so we could live in peace.

Gemma Cunningham (6) St Ann's Sunday School, Rainhill, Merseyside.

November 12th
Dear Lord, please can you try and help us to stop the wars, to stop people from getting killed, and help your world to settle peacefully.

Jenny Roddis (9) Riseley C of E Lower School, Bedfordshire.

November 13th
Dear Father, please help to stop wars all over the world. Help us to live in peace and harmony. Help us to think about other people and not just ourselves. Forgive me for all the bad and selfish things I have done. I ask this prayer in Jesus' name.

Natasha Briscoe (8) St Mark's C of E Primary School, Worsley Hall, Wigan, Lancashire.

November 14th
Dear Lord, thank you for all the lovely things you have made in the world. Thank you for houses to live in, and Lord please help those who haven't got a home and have to live in cardboard boxes. Please help people who live in countries where there is war going on so they keep safe. Please stop war soon. In Christ's name.
Jennifer Holden (8) St Thomas' Brownies, Ashton-in-Makerfield, Lancashire.

>We pray for all who are ill.
>>'O Lord, have pity on me, and heal me for I am sick' Psalm 6:2

November 15th
Dear Lord, please help the sick people in the world and give them money to buy medicine.
Simon Brown (8) Bearsden Primary School, Glasgow.

November 16th
Dear God, please help the ones who are sick, and make the doctors clever enough to make them better.
Kyle Walsh (6) St Gabriel's C of E School, Huyton, Merseyside.

November 17th

Dear God, other people in the world are not as fortunate as me, and I would like people to have all the medical things they need. I had a problem with my eyes; I had an operation on them and they are now better. Thank you.

Hannah Peddel (8) Riseley C of E Lower School, Bedfordshire.

November 18th

Dear Lord, please could you heal all those people in hospital who have had surgery. Thank you for all the kindness and peace in the world.

Jade Milne (8) Newsham JMI School, Newsham, Preston, Lancashire.

November 19th

Dear Lord, please look after the children and adults who haven't got homes and are hungry and ill. Help those who are sad and feel left out and make them feel part of your special family.

Alexandra Page (7) All Saints' Church, Salterhebble, Halifax, West Yorkshire.

November 20th
Thank you God for all the world. I want to help the hungry people who have no food, and the people that are blind who have no guide dogs.

Gemma Johnson (5) 3rd Huyton Rainbow Unit, Huyton, Merseyside.

We give thanks for doctors, nurses and dentists:

November 21st
Dear Jesus, I pray for all children who are ill.
Help them to be brave and patient and to get better quickly. Please help all the people who look after us when we are ill, especially doctors and nurses.
Thank you for the gift of good health.

Kelly Lawless (8) 9th Warrington St Elphin's Brownies, Cheshire.

November 22nd
Dear God, thank you for my dentist for making my teeth better.

Carl Parr (6) St Mary's & St Thomas' C of E Primary School, St Helens, Merseyside.

November 23rd
Heavenly Father, we thank you for people you have healed, and at this very moment we are thinking of people whom we know and praying that you will heal them.

Hayley Zurawel (8) Riseley C of E School, Bedfordshire.

   and for our bodies:

November 24th
Dear Jesus, thank you for my legs so I can run and play with my friends. Help me to remember girls and boys who can't talk and need our help.

Andrew Hall (6) St James' Sunday School, Chapelthorpe, West Yorkshire.

November 25th
Dear God, thank you for making everyone. Thank you for giving me my brain.

Matthew Hubber (6) Matlock All Saints' Infants School, Matlock, Derbyshire.

November 26th
Dear God, I thank you for our hearing and seeing, and I thank you for our food. In Jesus' precious name.
Samantha Beard (6) St Bridget's Sunday School, Wavertree, Liverpool.

We pray for those who do not have clean water to drink:

November 27th
Dear Lord, I pray for all the people who are sick because of the dirty water they have to drink. I pray that soon they will have clean water so that they don't have the sickness so often. Lord, I wish to do this for you and to help them.
Samantha Rhodes (9) Riseley C of E Lower School, Bedfordshire.

and give thanks for places where the water is clean:

November 28th
Dear God, thank you for our clean water. Thank you for water to drink and water to wash our hands. Thank you for water for washing cars and our clothes.
Robert Bayton (6) Lightcliffe C of E School, Halifax, West Yorkshire.

and we thank God for Jesus:

> 'Wherever Jesus went he healed people'
> Matthew 9:35

November 29th
Dear God, thank you for Jesus who came down to earth and helped and healed all the crowds.
Sarah Kent (9) Holy Trinity Church, South Crosland, West Yorkshire.

> St Andrew is the patron saint of Scotland so today we have a prayer from Scotland.

November 30th
Dear Lord, please help me and my sisters and brothers and mummy and daddy to enjoy ourselves. Please look after us all, and thank you Lord for the whole world around us.
Bryony Bennison (8) St Mary-on-the-Rock Episcopal Church, Ellon, Aberdeenshire.

Chill *December* brings the sleet, Blazing fire, and Christmas treat

Now we are in the last month of the year, and it will not be long until Christmas, when we think about the birth of Jesus. (You can read all about it in Matthew 1 verses 18 to 25 and in Luke chapters 1 and 2.)

December 1st
Dear God, thank you for the days of the week and the weeks of the months. Thank you for the months of the year. And thank you for the special month of December, when we celebrate Christmas.
Maria Littley (7) St Peter's School, Pedmore, West Midlands.

With Christmas coming soon we give thanks for family life:

December 2nd
Dear God, I have my mum and dad, I have brothers and sisters. We all love Jesus, he lives with us in our home. And God is there, he is our Father. I have a bigger family at school and at church, where I have more brothers and sisters. I have a great big family with all God's children in the world. Thank you God for loving us all.
Joshua Tuthill (7) St Andrew's C of E School, Seaside, Eastbourne, East Sussex.

December 3rd
Dear God, watch over my family and keep them safe throughout the day. Bless our home and our work and may your love guide us always. Bless my parents and grandparents. Lord, hear my prayer.
Glenn Elmes (7) Tullow, Co. Carlow.

December 4th
Dear God, thank you for my mummy and daddy and my two brothers. Sometimes they fight and make me cry, but I still love them. Thank you for my friends and all the lovely flowers and trees.

Emily Pilkington (6) Waterfoot, Rossendale, Lancashire.

December 5th
We thank you Lord for sharing and caring, for fun and laughter, for family days out and the nice food we eat, and all the joys we find in our life together.

Emily Stelfox (7) St Anne's Church, Ings, Cumbria.

> Today is St Nicholas' day, the patron saint of children.
>> 'Jesus said, "Let the children come to me"'
>> Matthew 19:14

December 6th
Dear God, thank you for all the things you give us. Thank you for our toys and all our friends and thank you for making us. You have made us very happy for making all our friends and our mums and dads, our grandmas and grandpas. We love them very much and we love you as well.

Ffion Hales (6) Sywell C of E School, Northamptonshire.

December 7th
Thank you God for my mum and dad,
They are not really quite so bad.
Thank you for my little sister,
She really is a little miss.
Thank you for my brother,
He's not like any other.
Thank you that I know the way
To be with you, for good some day.
Sarah Cunningham (8) Shankill, Co. Dublin.

December 8th
Please God, bless dear Mummy, Daddy and my sister, grandmas and grandads, and make me a good girl, for Jesus Christ's sake.
Lucy Barnsley (6) All Saints' Sunday School, Elton, Derbyshire.

December 9th
Dear Lord, thank you for mothers who cuddle us when we are sad; for the warm happy smile upon her face, the beautiful blue eyes, the golden blonde hair. Dear Lord, thank you for mothers.
Jessica Stephenson (8) Christ Church, Denton, Lancashire.

December 10th

Dear God, thank you for the people in my family. My dad plays football with me. I like playing rugby. Please help me to be a good goalkeeper.

Christopher Preece (7) St Brides Major C in W Primary School, Mid Glamorgan.

December 11th

Dear Lord Jesus, bless my family and my friends. Help them to get through times of sadness. Let them understand all your words, lead them the right way to go and let them live their lives in peace and happiness. For Jesus' sake.

Deborah Gibson (8) Killeshandra, Co. Cavan.

But not everyone has a happy home and loving parents:

December 12th

Dear God, thank you for making families. Bless those who don't have mummies and daddies and please keep them safe. Thank you for all the things our parents give us. Help orphans know that their fathers and mothers are in heaven and that their parents still love them in every way. So no matter how old they are they know that they still have a proper mother and father in heaven with you. Please make their foster parents care and look after them in every way. This we ask through Jesus Christ our Lord.

Joanne Love (8) Christchurch Sunday School, Londonderry.

We thank God for making us able to move about:

December 13th

When I get up in the morning, thank you God for making my bones move.
When I get dressed, thank you God for making my bones move.
When I walk to school, thank you God for making my bones move.
When I play outside, thank you God for making my bones move.
When I eat my dinner, thank you God for making my bones move.
When I walk home, thank you God for making my bones move.

Natalie Rowe (8) Simonstone C of E School, Burnley, Lancashire.

As we come towards the end of another term, we give thanks for our school:

December 14th

Dear Jesus, thank you for books to read.

Samantha Ditchfield (4) Newburgh C of E School, Lancashire.

December 15th

Dear God, thank you for this term. Thank you for all our school work and thank you for looking after us.

Tamsin Hamid (8) Battyeford C of E School, West Yorkshire.

CHILDREN AT PRAYER 151

and for our church and youth groups:

December 16th
Dear Lord, we thank you for Explorers, Pathfinders, Scramblers and Climbers.
Nicola Biggins (7) St Paul's Explorers, Barrow-in-Furness, Cumbria.

December 17th
Dear God, thank you for Brownies, Guides, Beavers, Cubs and Scouts. Thank you for flowers, trees, animals, food, water and all nice things, and please make us worthy of you, Lord.
Nicola Huff (8) Wimbledon High School, London.

and for all people, whatever they are like:

December 18th
Dear Lord, please let us accept people with different colour skin. Please protect us, black or white. Please do not let us go against people with different colour skin so we may all live together in peace.
Emma Cox (9) 1st Charlwood Brownies, Horley, Surrey.

December 19th
Dear Lord, thank you that we are all different in lots of ways, even though some of us are disabled and have got cerebral palsy, or are blind and deaf. Thank you Lord for what we are.

Nicola Clode (9) 2nd Cleeve Brownies, Cleeve, Bristol, Avon.

December 20th
Dear Lord, I am sorry for all the things I have done wrong and for not being nice. Please forgive us when we pick on other people, and do not do what our mums ask us to do.

Manesh Lad (8) St Stephen & All Martyrs Cubs, Great Lever, Bolton, Lancashire.

We think about giving and receiving Christmas presents:

December 21st
Lord, I know I don't deserve anything such as Easter, Christmas and birthday presents. I know I've not been good enough for all these things. Please forgive me.

Laura Barrow (8) St Mary's Brownies, Widnes, Cheshire.

and all the things we enjoy in our own homes:

December 22nd

Dear God, thank you for my house that I live in
and for the clothes that keep me warm in the winter.
Thank you for the food I eat and the water I drink.
Thank you God for everything.

William Magowan (9) St Leonard's Parish Church, Walton le Dale, Preston, Lancashire.

especially when so many have almost nothing:

December 23rd

Dear Lord Jesus, thank you for clothes, food and
warmth. We are very sorry for those who die of
coldness; please help poor people to find warmth
and to find money to buy food. Thank you Jesus.

Heather Godwin (7) St Helen & St Giles, Rainham, Essex.

We think about Mary and Joseph travelling up to Bethlehem.

> 'A virgin will soon give birth to a son and he will be called Emmanuel, which means God with us'
> Isaiah 7:14

December 24th
Dear God, please help my mum because she is having a baby.
Robert Newton (7) Matlock All Saints' Infants School, Matlock, Derbyshire.

> 'And while they were there she gave birth to her first-born son, and she wrapped him in swaddling cloths and laid him in a manger, because there was no room for them in the inn.' Luke 2:7

December 25th – Christmas Day
Dear God, thank you for Sunday and Christmas, because Sunday is rest day and Christmas is our Lord Jesus's birthday.
Sian Yarwood Smith (7) St Peter's School, Pedmore, West Midlands.

December 26th
Dear God, thank you for Christ. Thank you for Christmas dinner. Thank you for my Christmas toys.
Paul Parr (5) Longview CP School, Huyton, Merseyside.

December 27th

Christmas is the time of year
For no more war and no more tears
For peace and love throughout the world
For every girl and boy.

Christmas is the time of year
To share with those we hold most dear.
Christmas is a time for fun,
For love and joy for everyone.

Calum McKenzie (9) Park Grove School, York.

December 28th

Dear Lord, thank you for children, jolly, happy and kind. They'll cheer you up when you're down, so never frown at a child. Dear Lord, thank you for children.

Jessica Stephenson (8) Christ Church, Denton, Lancashire.

December 29th

Dear God, thank you for the lovely games and things we can do today which other children couldn't do hundreds of years ago.

Clifford Harris (9) St James' Sunday School, Hayton, Aspatria, Cumbria.

December 30th

Dear Lord, thank you for providing our food – we must try to help others who are less fortunate than ourselves.

    Lord, in your mercy: Hear our prayer.

Dear Lord, please help us to love one another. Make countries more friendly with other countries. Help us to play our part in bringing peace to the world.

    Lord, in your mercy: Hear our prayer.

Dear Lord, there are many lonely people in this world, help us to look out for anyone who may need our friendship. Help us to love and care for them.

    Lord, in your mercy: Hear our prayer.

Dear Lord, let us pray for all the people who are not feeling well today, especially those who are in hospital. Give them your strength to face their illness.

    Lord, in your mercy: Hear our prayer.

Dear Lord, we remember those who have died. Welcome them into your Heaven and give them everlasting peace. Help everyone to know the joy of your love.

    Merciful Father: Accept these prayers for the sake of your Son, our Saviour, Jesus Christ. Amen.

The Beavers, St Paul's Church, Alverthorpe, West Yorkshire.

> 'Whatever you do or say, let it be in the name of the Lord Jesus' Colossians 3:17

December 31st

Dear Lord, thank you for making everything. Thank you for sending your only Son down to earth to be with us and die for us. Please help us to put you first, this year and the years to come.

Frances Oliver (9) Holy Trinity Church Club, Wednesfield Heath, West Midlands.

Index

CHILDREN
Babies Feb 3, Feb 6, Dec 24
Blind Nov 20, Dec 19
Cerebral palsy Dec 19
Deaf Dec 19
Different skin Dec 18
Dying Feb 21, Nov 7, Nov 11, Dec 30
Foster children Mar 30, Dec 12
Friends Feb 22, Apr 21, Apr 27, Apr 29, May 28, Jun 26, Jun 27, Jun 28, Aug 3, Aug 14, Aug 15, Sep 9, Sep 10, Dec 4, Dec 6
Handicapped Jan 23, Feb 18
Happy Feb 22, Sep 22, Dec 28
Hurt Feb 20
In hospital Jan 22, Jul 8, Nov 18
Nervous Feb 23
Orphans Jan 29, Mar 29, Dec 12
Sick Jan 21, Nov 15, Nov 16, Nov 17, Nov 19, Nov 21, Nov 23, Nov 27

CHURCH
Choirs Mar 20
Church bells May 1
Church building Mar 22, July 15, July 17, Sep 21
Clergy and ministers Mar 18, Mar 21, May 30, July 15
Conscience Mar 16
Easter Apr 15, Dec 21
Fellowship Mar 22, Mar 23, Apr 15
God's love Feb 28, Jun 30, Sep 15, Sep 16, Sep 17
Good Friday Apr 10, Apr 11, Apr 12, Apr 14
Holy Spirit May 31
Jesus Mar 24, Apr 9, Apr 10, Apr 11, Apr 12, Apr 13, Apr 14, May 21, Sep 15, Nov 1, Nov 2, Nov 3, Nov 4, Nov 5, Nov 29, Dec 2, Dec 25, Dec 26, Dec 31
Learning about God Feb 19, Mar 19, May 29, May 30, May 31
Missionaries Mar 21
Praying and singing Feb 2, Mar 19, Mar 20, Mar 22,

Mar 30, Apr 24, Apr 27, Aug 26, Aug 28, Nov 4, Nov 5
Sunday School Jan 11, Mar 7, Mar 18
Worship May 2, Nov 1

FAMILY
Adoption Mar 26
Arguments Apr 9
Aunts, uncles, cousins Feb 18
Broken homes and relationships Sep 29
Brothers and sisters Mar 30, Mar 31, Aug 1, Aug 2, Aug 8, Aug 10, Aug 11, Aug 12, Aug 13, Sep 13, Sep 21, Oct 24, Nov 30, Dec 2, Dec 4, Dec 7, Dec 8
Keep them safe Jan 7, Feb 8, Feb 28, Mar 27, Dec 3, Dec 11
Family tree Feb 6
Grandparents Feb 6, Feb 11, Feb 12, Mar 30, Jul 9, Aug 8, Aug 9, Dec 3, Dec 6, Dec 8
Great-grandparents Feb 13
Happiness Feb 29, Dec 27, Dec 28
Homes Mar 31, Aug 23, Dec 22
Ill Mar 25, Jul 8, Dec 30
Loving and kind Jan 14, Mar 14, Mar 26, Apr 29, Dec 28
Mums and dads Feb 6, Feb 9, Feb 10, Feb 15, Feb 16, Mar 14, Mar 25, Mar 30, Mar 31, Jul 9, Aug 1, Aug 3, Aug 4, Aug 7, Aug 10, Sep 13, Nov 30, Dec 2, Dec 3, Dec 4, Dec 6, Dec 7, Dec 8, Dec 9, Dec 10, Dec 12, Dec 24
One parent Mar 28
Teenagers Feb 6
Thank you Feb 7, Mar 23, Apr 17, Jul 3, Jul 8, Jul 9, Dec 28
Unemployed Mar 27

GROUPS AND ORGANIZATIONS
Brownies, Guides, Scouts, Cubs, Rainbows, Beavers, Rangers Jan 19, Jul 27, Jul 28, Dec 17
Explorers, Pathfinders, Scramblers and Climbers Dec 16

HELP US
Be brave Jan 5, Feb 25, Dec 11
Be good and kind Jan 10, Mar 14, Sep 14
Be good friends Feb 26

Be helpful Apr 25, Apr 26, Apr 27
Be polite Apr 26
Be tidy Feb 25, Mar 7
Care for others Jan 4, Feb 21, Apr 25, Sep 8
Do better work Jan 10, Jun 14, Jun 16, Jun 17, Jun 18
Keep calm Feb 26
Not always have own way Jun 9, Jun 10
Not to do wrong things Jan 3, Mar 11, Apr 27, Apr 28, Apr 29, Nov 5, Dec 20
Not have nightmares Aug 27
Say sorry Mar 12, Mar 13, Mar 14, Mar 15, Mar 16, Aug 1, Dec 20
Say thank you Mar 31
School Feb 24, Jun 12, Jun 13, Jun 14, Jun 15, Jun 16, Jun 17, Jun 18, Jun 20, Jun 22, Jun 25, Sep 8, Sep 9, Sep 12, Dec 15
Those I love Feb 20
To do what is best Feb 19, Dec 31
To learn Feb 19, May 31, Jun 13, Jun 16, Jun 17, Jun 18, Jun 20
To listen Feb 27, Jun 14

PLEASE
Bless and protect us Sep 3
Forgive Mar 11, Mar 13, Mar 15, Mar 16, Apr 22, Aug 1, Aug 27, Nov 5, Nov 13, Dec 20, Dec 21
Help me to love Feb 14, Jun 9, Sep 14, Sep 17
Help me to please you Jan 25, Dec 31
Help me to share Mar 30
Keep us safe Jan 2, Mar 27, Apr 23
Keep my family safe Jan 7, Feb 8
Look after my mum and dad Feb 15, Feb 16, Feb 18
Look after my grandparents Feb 17, Feb 18
World peace Jan 8, Mar 3, Apr 17, Apr 18, Apr 19, Apr 20, Apr 21, Apr 22, Nov 6, Nov 8, Nov 9, Nov 10, Nov 11, Nov 12, Nov 13, Nov 14, Dec 30

SCHOOL AND SUNDAY SCHOOL
Books Dec 14
Difficult days Jun 25, Sep 10
Dinner ladies Jun 16
Exams and tests Jun 17, Jun 18, Jun 19

Friends Feb 22, Feb 26, May 28, Jun 14, Jun 15, Jun 16, Jun 26, Jun 27, Jun 28, Jul 15, Jul 16, Sep 9, Sep 10, Sep 12, Sep 25
In class Feb 24, Feb 27, Jun 14, Jun 16, Jun 17, Jun 18, Jun 20, Jun 21, Sep 8, Sep 11, Sep 12, Dec 15
Playground Jun 22, Jun 23, Sep 9
Sharing Feb 25, May 31
School Trips Jun 24
Teachers Jan 11, Mar 7, Mar 18, May 28, May 29, Jun 12, Jun 13, Jun 16, Sep 13, Sep 25, Dec 15

SPECIAL DAYS AND PEOPLE
Birthdays Jul 29, Jul 30, Jul 31, Dec 21
Christian Aid week May 14
Christmas Sep 1, Dec 1, Dec 21, Dec 25, Dec 26, Dec 27
Good Friday Apr 10, Apr 11, Apr 12
Easter Apr 15, Apr 16, Dec 21
Harvest and seedtime Apr 3, Aug 29, Aug 30, Sep 1, Sep 18, Sep 19, Sep 22
St Andrew Nov 30
St David Mar 1
St George Apr 23
St Patrick Mar 17
St Joseph of Arimathea Apr 11
St Simon of Cyrene Apr 11
St Valentine Feb 14
The Queen Apr 23

THANK YOU for
Animals and pets Jan 26, Apr 5, Apr 16, Apr 17, May 4, May 5, May 6, Aug 2, Sep 2, Sep 3, Sep 4, Sep 5, Oct 3, Oct 5, Oct 7, Oct 8, Oct 10, Oct 11, Oct 12, Oct 13, Oct 14, Oct 15, Oct 16, Oct 17, Oct 18, Oct 19, Oct 20
Artists May 25
Birds Apr 1, Apr 7, May 4, Jul 4, Jul 5, Jul 6, Jul 9, Sep 2, Sep 3, Sep 6, Nov 5
Bodies Jan 13, Jul 10, Sep 6, Sep 7, Nov 24, Nov 25, Nov 26, Dec 13
Builders and bricklayers May 25
Cars Aug 21, Aug 22, Nov 28
Clothes Apr 30, Aug 26, Sep 23, Nov 28, Dec 22
Coal May 4
Colours Mar 6, May 5, May 6, Jul 5
Church Jan 11, Feb 2, Jul 15, Jul 17, Jul 28, Sep 18, Sep 21

CHILDREN AT PRAYER

Days of the week Jul 1, Dec 1
Dentists Nov 22
Doctors and nurses May 26, Jul 8, Nov 16, Nov 17, Nov 18, Nov 21
Families Feb 7, Feb 8, Mar 18, Mar 23, Mar 29, Mar 31, Apr 17, May 29, Jul 3, Jul 10, Jul 15, Aug 1, Aug 2, Aug 3, Aug 4, Aug 5, Aug 7, Aug 8, Aug 9, Aug 25, Sep 21, Oct 2, Oct 9, Oct 31, Nov 30, Dec 2, Dec 3, Dec 10, Dec 11, Dec 12
Farmers Apr 4, Sep 19, Sep 22, Sep 30
Firemen May 26
Fishermen May 25, Aug 30
Flowers and plants Apr 1, Apr 3, Apr 4, Apr 16, Apr 17, May 4, May 7, May 9, Sep 2, Sep 3, Sep 4, Sep 6, Sep 18, Sep 19, Sep 21, Nov 5
Food and drink Jan 30, Feb 5, Mar 17, Apr 30, May 14, May 23, May 24, Jul 5, July 6, Jul 7, Jul 9, Jul 28, Jul 30, Jul 31, Sep 18, Sep 23, Oct 8, Oct 31, Nov 3, Nov 26, Nov 28, Dec 22, Dec 23, Dec 30
Friends Jan 17, Mar 23, Mar 29, Apr 17, May 29, Jun 26, Jun 27, Jun 30, Jul 17, Jul 27, Jul 28, Jul 30, Aug 14
Fun and games Jun 1, Jun 2, Jun 3, Jun 4, Jun 5, Jun 6, Jun 7, Aug 15, Aug 16, Aug 17, Aug 18, Aug 20
Happy times Jan 16, Jul 15, Sep 22
Harvest and seedtime Apr 3, Aug 29, Aug 30, Sep 1, Sep 18, Sep 19, Sep 22
Health Aug 19
Help when ill Jan 31, Nov 17, Dec 30
Homes Jan 18, Feb 5, Mar 18, May 25, Jul 10, Jul 15, Jul 17, Aug 23, Aug 25, Sep 28, Oct 31, Dec 22
Hospitals Jul 8, Nov 16, Nov 17, Nov 18
Insects May 9, Jul 4, Jul 5, Sep 2, Sep 21, Oct 3
Jesus Mar 24, Apr 10, Apr 12, Apr 13, Apr 14, May 21, Jun 29, Aug 3, Nov 1, Nov 2, Nov 3, Nov 4, Nov 5, Nov 29, Dec 2, Dec 25, Dec 26
Life Feb 1
Light Apr 16
Lighthouses May 27
Love Jan 6, Mar 17, Jul 16
Lovely day Jan 15, Apr 1
Months of the year Jan 31, Dec 1

New baby Jan 9, Dec 24
Night Mar 17
Oil May 4
Paper May 4
Policemen May 26
Presents Jul 30, Jul 31
Rest Mar 17
School May 28, May 29, Jun 12, Jun 13, Jun 15, Jun 16, Jun 20, Jun 21, Jun 24, Jul 15, Jul 16, Sep 8, Sep 9, Sep 11, Sep 12, Oct 31
Seasons Mar 2, Sep 1, Oct 1
Senses Jul 6
Sports Jun 1, Jun 2, Jun 3, Jun 8, Jul 15, Aug 15, Aug 16, Aug 19, Aug 23, Dec 10
Sunday Jan 12, Dec 25
Sunny and rainy days Jan 1, Jun 1, Jul 12, Jul 13
Talents May 25
Toys and games Mar 31, Jul 17, Aug 16, Aug 17, Aug 18, Aug 20, Aug 23, Aug 24, Oct 31, Dec 26, Dec 29
The world Jan 31, Mar 23, Apr 2, Apr 4, Apr 16, May 3, May 11, May 13, Jun 4, Jul 2, Jul 11, Aug 31, Oct 5, Oct 31, Nov 6, Nov 20
TV and radio May 26, Aug 18
Vets Oct 29

THE WORLD
Animals Jan 28, Mar 8, Apr 5, Apr 16, Apr 27, Apr 28, May 4, May 5, May 6, May 19, Jul 4, Jul 6, Jul 8, Jul 17, Aug 30, Sep 2, Sep 21, Sep 25, Oct 3, Oct 5, Oct 7, Oct 8, Oct 10, Oct 11, Oct 12, Oct 13, Oct 14, Oct 15, Oct 16, Oct 17, Oct 18, Oct 19, Oct 20, Oct 21, Oct 22, Oct 23, Oct 24, Oct 25, Oct 26, Oct 27, Oct 28, Oct 29, Oct 30, Oct 31
Autumn Mar 2, Sep 1, Oct 1
Beach Mar 8
Birds Mar 4, Apr 1, Apr 7, May 4, May 12, Jul 4, Jul 5, Jul 6, Jul 9, Sep 2, Oct 2, Nov 5
Blind Nov 20, Dec 19
Bombs Apr 18
Care for living things Jan 27
Cars Mar 7, May 8
Cold countries May 10
Countryside May 10, Jul 12
Crime and violence May 22
Desert May 10
Dumping rubbish Jan 28, Mar 7, Mar 8, Mar 9, Apr 8, Oct 2
Dying and dead Jan 24, Apr 20, Nov 7, Nov 10, Nov 11
Famine Apr 17, Apr 22, Sep 27, Nov 7, Nov 20

Farmers and farming Apr 4, May 19, Aug 30, Sep 19, Sep 30, Oct 8

Fish Apr 8, Oct 2, Oct 4, Oct 20

Flowers Apr 3, Apr 4, Apr 16, Apr 17, May 1, Jul 4, Jul 5, Jul 6, Jul 9, Sep 2, Sep 18, Sep 19, Sep 21, Sep 24

Food and drink Apr 1, Apr 22, May 14, May 15, May 16, May 17, May 18, May 19, May 20, Jul 3, Jul 5, Jul 6, Jul 7, Jul 9, Aug 30, Sep 18, Sep 19, Sep 22, Sep 23, Sep 24, Sep 27, Sep 28, Oct 8, Nov 26, Nov 28, Dec 22, Dec 23, Dec 30

Fruit Jul 6, Jul 7, Sep 18, Sep 22

Grass May 9, Sep 26

Homeless Jan 29, Feb 4, Apr 20, May 22, May 31, Sep 28, Nov 14, Nov 19, Dec 23

Acknowledgements

Many thanks to all Mothers' Union Diocesan Presidents and Unit Directors of the Diocesan Prayer and Spirituality departments whose efforts ensured such a good response from churches, schools, groups and organizations in England, Wales, Scotland and Ireland. Many thanks to all who responded so willingly and produced such a wealth of material. Particular mention must be made of Liverpool diocese, whose well-organized prayer competition produced hundreds of entries, a number of which are included in *Children at Prayer*, and to the Province of Ireland and the diocese of Chichester who sent in their own books of prayer produced for the Year of the Family.

Thanks also to all at the Mothers' Union headquarters at Mary Sumner House for their help and encouragement, especially the Marketing and Prayer & Spirituality departments. If this book proves to fulfil a need it is hoped to produce a further one for young people of 9 to 16 years.